CW01160055

# The Junior Encyclopaedia of Islam

Saniyasnain Khan
Mohammad Imran Erfani

Goodwordkidz

First published 2003
Reprinted 2004, 2006
© Goodword Books 2006

Goodword Books Pvt. Ltd.
A 21, Sector 4, Noida, UP 201 301
E-mail: info@goodwordbooks.com
Printed in India

**www.goodwordbooks.com**

# Contents

| | |
|---|---|
| An Introduction to Islam | 4 |
| What is Islam? | 4 |
| What do Muslims believe? | 4 |
| Who was the Prophet Muhammad? | 5 |
| What is the Qur'an? | 7 |
| What is the Kabah? | 8 |
| How do Muslims practice their faith? | 9 |
| Why are modern numerals called "Arabic numerals"? | 10 |
| Arabic Writing | 11 |
| World's Muslim populations | 11 |
| What is *jihad*? | 12 |
| The Islamic Calendar | 13 |
| Ten Masterpieces of Classical Islamic Art | 14 |
| A-Z Fact Finder | 17 |
| Life of the Prophet Muhammad ﷺ | 65 |
| Doing *wudu* or ablutions for prayer | 69 |
| How to say your prayers | 74 |
| Names of surahs in the Qur'an | 85 |
| 99 Beautiful Names of Allah | 89 |
| Names of the Prophet Muhammad ﷺ | 93 |
| English names/words and their Arabic equivalents/meaning | 96 |
| Adhan or Call to Prayer | 98 |
| Chronology of Islam | 99 |
| Notable Muslims | 105 |
| Suggestions for Reading | 111 |
| Prayers from the Quran | 120 |
| Prayers from the Hadith | 128 |
| Important Phrases | 133 |
| Short Surahs | 134 |

# AN INTRODUCTION TO ISLAM

## What is Islam?

Islam is the religion, and the way of life, of about one fifth of the world's population. Its adherents, called Muslims, believe Islam is Allah's final message to humankind, a reconfirmation and perfection of the messages that Allah has revealed through earlier prophets.

## What do Muslims believe?

The central Muslim belief is that there is only one God, unique, incomparable, eternal, absolute and without peer or associate. He cannot be perceived in this world but through His works.

Other important tenets of Islam are that Allah is the Creator of all that exists; that His will is supreme; that He has sent messengers to humankind, to whom Muhammad was the "seal"—that is, the last; that the Qur'an is the very Word of Allah; that angels, immortal creatures, exist, as does Satan; that humans are responsible to Allah for their actions; and that, on Judgement Day, the all-knowing and merciful Allah will judge all mortals according to their deeds in this life.

# Who was the Prophet Muhammad?

Muhammad was the prophet through whom, Allah sent His last revelation to humankind.

Muhammad was born around the year 570 AD in the Arabian city of Makkah, a city built on trade and on the flow of pilgrims to the Ka'bah, the shrine believed to have been erected by Adam, and which was then filled with idols from many cultures.

Muhammad was orphaned at the age of six. In his 20's, he went to work for a widow named Khadijah, who ran trading caravans. Working for her, he travelled widely and earned a reputation for trustworthiness. Later, and in spite of a considerable age difference, he married Khadijah.

In his late 30's, Muhammad took to meditating alone in a cave on Mount Hira, a few hours' walk outside the city. There, one day during the month of Ramadan, he heard a voice ordering him to "Recite!"

Three times, Muhammad replied that he could not: He was illiterate. But each time the command was repeated, and finally Muhammad received the first revelation:

Recite: In the name of your Lord who created, created man from a clot. Recite: And your Lord is Most Bounteous, Who taught by the pen, Taught man that which he knew not.

The voice—it revealed itself as the Angel Gabriel—told Muhammad that he was to be the Messenger of Allah, and the revelations continued at irregular intervals for the 22 remaining years of Muhammad's life. The total of these revelations is the Qur'an, a word that means, literally, "recitation."

At first, Muhammad told only his wife and his closest friends of his experience. But as the revelations kept coming they enjoined him to proclaim the oneness of Allah publicly—something that took courage, because most Makkans believed there were many gods (polytheism).

It was the eloquence of the revelations, and the ease with which listeners recognised in them true words of Allah, that led to the emergence of Muslims. But Muhammad also faced opposition from Makkan polytheists: To htem, Muhammad's monotheism was a threat to their control of the Ka'bah—and the pilgrimage trade. In the early fall of 622, Muhammad and his followers emigrated from Makkah north to the town of Yathrib (later renamed al-Madinah). This emigration— known as the *hijrah*—marks the beginning of the Islamic calendar, because it was in Yathrib that the followers of Muhammad's teachings developed a society organised along the reformist lines of Allah's revelations.

In 630, after few battles, Muhammad peacefully re-entered Makkah, where he cleared the Ka'bah of idols. Two years later, he took ill and died on June 8, 632. His close companion, Abu Bakr al-Siddiq, told the grieving Muslim community, "Whoever worshipped Muhammad, let him know that Muhammad is dead, but whoever worships Allah, let him know that Allah lives, and dies not."

## What is the Qur'an?

The Qur'an is the holy book of Islam. Muslims believe that it is the Word of Allah, transmitted by the Angel Gabriel, in Arabic, through the Prophet Muhammad. It is meant for all humanity, not for any exclusive group. At its heart is the teaching of monotheism, but the Qur'an provides guidance for every part of a believer's life, including aspects that in the West would be considered social, political or legal, and not religious. The Qur'an is considered by Muslims to complete Allah's earlier revelations.

Unlike the Bible, there is only one version of the Qur'an, unchanged since Muhammad received it. A number of his followers had carefully memorised each of the revelations, word for word—an achievement still common among serious scholars—and the text we know today was written down by the year 651. The Qur'an is also considered to be untranslatable, because no other language carries the full range of often subtle meaning that the Arabic of the Qur'an can convey. Thus Muslim scholars regard versions of the Qur'an in other languages to be interpretations rather than true translations, and in Arabic literature there is no work whose eloquence, clarity and erudition approach those of the Qur'an.

# What is the Kabah?

The Kabah is the black cubical stone structure in the courtyard of the Great Mosque at Makkah. It was built by the prophet Ibrahim (Abraham) and his son Ismail (Ishmael). The Kabah is empty, and it is not entered except for a ritual cleaning each year. A black cloth covering, called the *Kiswah*, embroidered in gold with Qur'anic calligraphy, is made for it each year. When Muslims pray, wherever in the world they are, it is the direction of the Kabah that they face. During the Hajj, pilgrims circle the Kabah seven times in a ritual called the *tawaf*, or circumambulation, which is also performed throughout the rest of the year.

## How do Muslims practice their faith?

*Islam*, in Arabic, means "submission," meaning submission to the will of Allah. It also means "peace," the peace one finds through submission of Allah's will. Muslims accept five primary obligations, commonly called the "Five Pillars of Islam." In practice, of course, Muslims can be seen observing all of these to varying degrees, for the responsibility of fulfilling the obligations lies on the shoulders of each individual.

**The profession of faith (*shahadah*):** This is a simple statement: "There is no god but Allah; Muhammad is the Messenger of Allah,"

**Prayer (*salah*):** Muslims pray five times a day—at dawn, noon, afternoon, sunset and evening—facing toward the Ka'bah, the House of Allah, in the Great Mosque in Makkah. They may pray wherever they are when prayer-time arrives, in any clean place, preferable in the company of other Muslims. On Fridays at noon, Muslims are encouraged to pray as a gathered community in congregational mosques. There is a sequence of physical postures, fixed by tradition, for ritual prayer, and the prayers are said in Arabic regardless of the local language.

**Charity (*zakah*):** A fixed proportion of a Muslim's net worth—not just his or her income—is prescribed as a donation for the welfare of the community, whether that community is made up of Muslims, non-Muslims or a mixture.

**Fasting (*sawm*):** Every day from dawn to dusk during the holy month of Ramadan, Muslims must abstain from eating, drinking, smoking and sexual contact; even more than at other times, they must also avoid cursing, lying, cheating, and otherwise abusing or harming others.

**Pilgrimage (*Hajj*):** The journey to Makkah is obligatory for every able-bodied Muslim who can afford to make it. Pilgrimage need be made only once in a lifetime, but it can be made several times if a Muslim wishes. The *hajj* proper is made between the 8th and 13th days of *Dhu al-Hijjah*, the 12th month of the Islamic calendar, and every pilgrim carries out specified rituals at specific times. At any other time of year, Muslims can perform similar prayers and rituals and thus complete *'Umrah*, or "lesser pilgrimage."

## Why are modern numerals called "Arabic numerals"?

The modern numerals widely used today were probably developed in India, but it was Arabs who transmitted this system to the West. In 71, an Indian scholar arrived in Baghdad bringing with him a treatise on astronomy that used the Indian numerical system, which the Arabs admired because it was more economical than the roman system. In time, they added a further improvement: the *sifr* ("cipher"), or zero.

## Arabic Writing

Most scholars believe that Arabic developed from Nabataean and/or Aramaic dialects spoken in northern Arabia and much of the Levant during roughly a thousand years before the Islamic era.

The Arabic alphabet has 28 letters. More complex than differing capital and small letters in English, each Arabic letter may have up to four forms, depending on where it appears in the word and which letters precede or follow it. The Arabic script is read from right to left.

The cursive nature of the script and the variability of the letterforms made it difficult to adapt Arabic for use with early printing presses. It is for this reason that the Arab world continued for some centuries after the time of Gutenberg to rely on handwriting for the production of books, especially the Qur'an. This was one of the reasons that calligraphy—"beautiful writing"—emerged as perhaps the most important Arab art form.

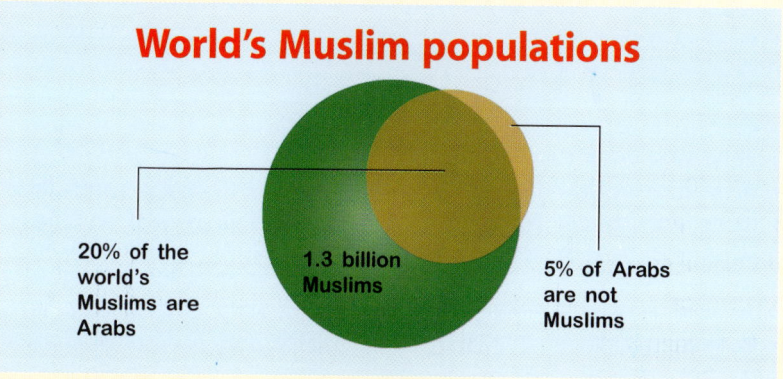

### World's Muslim populations

20% of the world's Muslims are Arabs

1.3 billion Muslims

5% of Arabs are not Muslims

## What is *jihad*?

The term *jihad* in Arabic connotes "to struggle or strive"—to exert oneself to the utmost to achieve one's goal. Since the early Muslims had to strive hard during wars with aggressors, these wars came, in an extended sense, to be called *jihad*. The actual word for war in Arabic is *qital*, not *jihad*. War with an aggressor is a chance occurrence, taking place as warranted by particular situations, while *jihad* is a continuos action which is at the core of the believer's life day in and day out. It is an ongoing process.

This constant *jihad* means strict adherence to the will of God in all aspects of one's life, and the prevention of any obstacle coming in the way of fulfilling God's will—for instance, the desires of the self, the urge to serve one's own interests, the compulsion of social traditions, the need for compromises, ego problems, greed for wealth, etc. All these thing directly thwart righteous actions. Overcoming all such hurdles and persevering in obeying God's commands are the real *jihad*. Thus, *jihad* is meant to guard against evils that can lead a person astray either because of his selfishness or prejudices. Its role is mainly corrective vis-à-vis one's own life.

Essentially *jihad* is a peaceful struggle. One form of this peaceful struggle is *dawah*—presenting the message of Islam to the non-Muslims. This kind of *jihad* is called in the Qur'an as "the greater *jihad*".

# The Islamic Calendar

The Islamic calendar is based on a lunar year of 12 full lunar cycles taking exactly 354 and 11/30 days. Each new year in the Islamic calendar thus begins 10 or 11 days earlier in the 364¼-day solar calendar commonly used in the West. The 12 months of the Islamic year are:

Muharram, Safar, Rabi' al-Awwal ("Rabi' I"), Rabi' al-Thani ("Rabi' II"), Jumada al-Ula ("Jumada I"), Jumada al-Akhirah ("Jumada II"), Rajab, Sha'ban, Ramadan, Shawwal, Dhu al-Qa'dah, and Dhu al-Hijjah.

The first day of year one of the Islamic calendar was set as the first day of the *hijrah*, the Prophet's move from Makkah to Madinah: July 26, 622. The western convention is designating Islamic dates is thus by the abbreviation AH, which stands for the Latin *anno hegirae*, or "Year of the Hegira."

To roughly convert an Islamic calendar year (AH) into a Gregorian equivalent (AD), or vice versa, use one of the following equations:

$$AD = 622 + (32/33 \times AH)$$

$$AH = 33/32 \times (AD - 622)$$

# Ten Masterpieces of Classical Islamic Art

"Great nations write their autobiographies in three manuscripts, the book of their deeds, the book of their words and the book of their art," wrote Ruskin. "Of the three the only trustworthy one is the last." The objects listed below, chosen by historians of Islamic art Jonathan M. Bloom and Sheila S. Blair, are only 10 pages from the vast "manuscript" of Islamic civilization, but they offer a sample of the riches of the whole.

1. **The Dome of the Rock,** Jerusalem, 692. The first great work of Islamic architecture. It was built over the rock from which the Prophet Muhammad made his miraculous ascent to heaven, which is described in chapter 17 of the Qur'an.

2. **The Malwiya minaret,** Samarra, Iraq, mid-ninth century. This 50-meter (160') helicoidal tower of sun-dried and baked brick was probably modelled on ancient ziggurats. It symbolizes the power of Islam at the zenith of the Baghdad-based Abbasid caliphate.

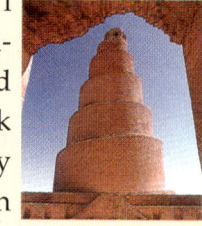

3. **The Mughira pyxis,** carved at Cordoba, Spain, 968. This small, exquisite box, carved from a cylindrical section of elephant tusk, is the most beautiful of the handful of known Islamic ivory carvings. Now it is in the Louvre in Paris.

4. **The *minbar* from Kutubiyyah Mosque,** Marrakesh, Morocco, 1137.

This wooden pulpit, nearly four meters (13') tall, was carved in Cordoba by the descendants of the workmen who carved out Mughira pyxis. Hundreds of thousands of pieces of wood and bone are carved and fitted together with consummate artistry.

**5. The *mihrab* from Maydan Mosque,** Kashan, Iran, 1226. (A *mihrab* is a niche in a wall of a mosque indicating the direction of the Ka'bah.) Composed of glazed ceramic slabs fitted into a complex, harmonious ensemble of calligraphy and arabesques, this is the acme of the difficult luster technique of overglaze decoration perfected by Persian ceramists. Now it is in the Islamic Museum of Berlin.

**6. The Baptistere of Saint-Louis,** Cairo, 1300. This hammered bronze basin, inlaid in silver and gold, is decorated on both the interior and the exterior with marvelous figural scenes showing hunters, servants, and warriors. First made to catch water after hand-washing before prayers, it was later used only as a baptismal font by the French court. Now it is in the Louvre Museum in Paris.

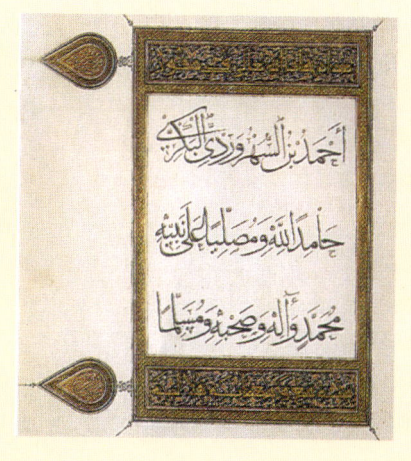

**7. The Ahmad al-Suhrawardi Qur'an manuscript,** Baghdad, 1307. This is arguably the finest display of the calligrapher's art. The paper was polished to an impeccable smoothness, allowing the pen to glide effortlessly across a pearly surface. This was a multivolume manuscript for an anonymous patron, and it is now dispersed. The colophon is in the Metropolitan Museum of Art in New York.

8. **The Ardebil Carpets,** Iran, 1539-40. These two enormous carpets were worked in 10 colours of silk and wool. Each has more than 25 million knots, making them one of the most splendid examples of the weaver's art. This one is in the Victoria and Albert Museum, London; the other is in the Los Angeles County Museum of Art.

9. **The Selimiye Mosque,** Edirne, Turkey, 1574. The breathtaking interior of the mosque is the masterpiece of the Ottoman architect Sinan, who created a huge and uninterrupted space under a towering dome. The centralized space of the prayer hall literally and symbolically embraces the community of believers and unites them under the radiance of Allah.

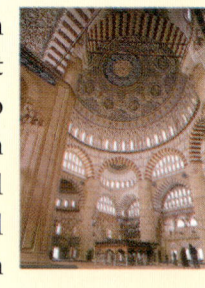

10. **The Taj Mahal,** Agra, India, 1647. This enormous white marble monument is set in a garden along the banks of the Jamuna river, centerpiece of complex designed to evoke the gardens of paradise that await believers.

*(Adapted from Saudi Aramco World)*

# A-Z Fact-Finder

# A

**'Abbas** The son of 'Abd al-Muttalib, who was the paternal uncle of the Prophet Muhammad. He was the founder of the Abbasid dynasty.

**'Abbasids** Major dynasty of the medieval Islamic period in Baghdad, whose founder was 'Abbas 'Abd al-Muttalib.

**'Abd** Servant (of Allah).

**'Abd Allah ibn 'Abd al-Muttalib** Father of the Prophet Muhammad. He died before the birth of the Prophet.

**'Abd Allah ibn Muhammad** Son of the Prophet Muhammad and Khadijah bint Khuwaylid. He died in infancy.

**'Abd al-Malik ibn Marwan** The fifth caliph of the Umayyad dynasty.

**'Abd al-Muttalib ibn Hashim** Father of 'Abdullah and the paternal grandfather of the Prophet Muhammad.

**'Abd al-'Uzza** An ancestor of the Prophet Muhammad.

**'Abd al-'Uzza ibn 'Abd al-Muttalib** Uncle of the Prophet Muhammad, who vehemently opposed the Prophet. He was also known as Abu Lahab.

**'Abd Manaf** Father of Hashim and an ancestor of the Prophet Muhammad.

**a** b c d e f g h i j k l m n o p q r s t u v w x y z

**'Abd Shams** Ancestor of the Prophet Muhammad, son of 'Abd Manaf and father of Umayya.

**ablaq** Striped masonry in Islamic architecture.

**ablution** [See: WUDU]

**Abrahah** A ruler of Yaman or governor of Abyssinia in South Arabia. He organised an attack on the Ka'bah, which failed.

**Abraham** [See: IBRAHIM]

**Abu Bakr** Father of Aishah, and the first *khalifah* to rule over the Islamic community after the death of the Prophet.

**Abu Dawud** One of the chief compilers of *hadith* (traditions).

**Abu Hurayrah** One of the companions of the Prophet and a narrator of a very great number of *hadith*.

**Abu Jahl** A member of the Makhzum clan of the Quraysh tribe, and a fierce opponent of the Prophet Muhammad.

**Abu Lahab** [See: 'ABD AL-'UZZA IBN 'ABD AL-MUTTALIB]

**Abu al-Qasim** *Kunya* or nickname of the Prophet.

**Abu Sufyan** A member of the 'Abd Shams of the Quraysh tribe.

**Abu Talib** Uncle of the Prophet Muhammad and the father of 'Ali Ibn Abi, Talib greatly helped the Prophet in his early days of prophethood.

**Abu 'Ubayda ibn al-Jarrah** One of the ten companions of the Prophet to whom paradise was promised. [See: ASHARA MUBASHSHRA]

**'Ad** An arrogant tribe of giants in the pre-Islamic period of the South Arabian region. They were killed by a terrible storm. They have been referred to in the Qur'an several times.

**a** b c d e f g h i j k l m n o p q r s t u v w x y z

**adab** Good manners; the refinement or good habits handed down over the centuries.

**Adam** The first man and the first prophet. The father of mankind, he had the title of *Safiyullah* or, the "chosen one of Allah".

**adhan** The call to prayer, which is made five times a day to the Muslim faithful by a *muadhdhin*.

**'Adn** Eden. One of the names of Paradise.

**Ahl al-Kahf** [See: ASHAB AL-KAHF]

**Ahl al-Kitab** The People of the Book: basically the Jews and Christians.

**Ahl al-Sunnah wa'l-Jama'ah** The People of Custom and Community, a title by which the Sunnis are known.

**Ahmad ibn Hanbal** Founder of the Hanbali School of Islamic Law.

**'A'ishah bint Abu Bakr** One of the wives of the Prophet and daughter of Abu Bakr. The Prophet died in her bedchamber and he was also buried there. 'A'ishah's contribution to the preserving of the *Hadith* was colossal, as she narrated over one thousand *ahadith* of the Prophet Muhammad.

**ajal** Moment of death or lifespan.

**akhbar** News, messages, information.

**al-Akhirah** 'Afterlife.' The eternal life after death, which will continue either in Paradise or in Hell, according to one's deeds.

**akhlaq** Morals, personal character.

**Alexandria** A major city in Egypt, founded by and named after Alexander the Great. It was famous for its lighthouse, which was one of the seven

**a** b c d e f g h i j k l m n o p q r s t u v w x y z

wonders of the ancient world.

**'Ali ibn Abi Talib** The fourth *khalifah* or caliph, who ruled over the Islamic community. He was the cousin of the Prophet Muhammad and later became his son-in-law as well, by marrying his daughter Fatimah.

**Allah** The name of the Creator of the Universe in the Qur'an. It literally means 'The God.'

**Allahu Akbar** 'Allah is Most Great.' A glorification of Allah often repeated in prayers.

**Alyasa** One of the name of the prophets mentioned in the Qur'an.

**al-Amin** 'The Trustworthy.' This was a title given to the Prophet Muhammad in his youth, before the revelations began.

**amin** The Arabic form of Amen, which means assent, "truly" and "so be it."

**Amina bint Wahb** The mother of the Prophet. She died when the Prophet was six years old.

**Amir al-Mu'minin** 'Commander of the Faithful.'

**'Amr ibn al-'As** He belonged to the Sahm clan of the Quraysh tribe. He embraced Islam before the Prophet's capture of Makkah and was sent by the Prophet to Oman. Later he was sent by Abu Bakr to Palestine. He was the founder of *al-Fustat* in Egypt.

**angel** The being created from light to praise, serve and obey Allah. Angels are invisible to the human eye.

**al-ansar** 'The Helpers.' This title was given to the people of Madinah for the help they gave to the Prophet Muhammad.

**a** b c d e f g h i j k l m n o p q r s t u v w x y z

**Anti-Christ** [See: AL-DAJJAL]

**apostle** [See: RASUL]

**'aqida** Faith, belief, doctrine, dogma.

**'aqiqah** A non-obligatory tradition of shaving the hair of a child on the seventh day after birth. At that time a sheep or a goat is sacrificed and the weight of the hair in silver is distributed among the poor.

**al-Aqsa, al-Masjid** 'The Furthest Mosque.' Also called *al-Bayt al-Muqaddas* or 'The Holy House', from which the Prophet made his *mi'raj*. Situated in Jerusalem, this is one of the most sacred mosques of Islam.

**Arabesque** A kind of decoration composed of leaves or other vegetal shapes designed in a coherent pattern. It is a common feature of Islamic Art.

**'Arafat** Situated about 13 miles from Makkah this plain is a major focal point for the *hajj*. On the ninth day of the Islamic month *Dhu al-Hijja*, pilgrims carry out the solemn rite of 'standing' (*wuquf*) at 'Arafat and a special sermon is preached. If the *wuquf* at 'Arafat is omitted, the entire pilgrimage is considered invalid.

**arkan** The word used in Arabic to refer to the five pillars of Islam. These are: *salah*, *sawm*, *zakah*, *shahadah* and *hajj*.

**'arsh** Throne.

**Asad** A clan of the Quraysh tribe, to which the Prophet's wife Khadijah belonged.

**Ascension of the Prophet** [See: MI'RAJ]

**ashab al-kahf** 'The Companions of the Cave.' This is a Quranic title frequently given to a group of youths who

**a** b c d e f g h i j k l m n o p q r s t u v w x y z

fell asleep in a cave and awoke many years later.

**ashab al-kisa'** A title given to the 'Four Perfect Women', namely, Asiyah—the wife of Pharaoh, Maryam—the mother of 'Isa, Khadijah—the wife of the Prophet Muhammad and Fatimah—the daughter of the Prophet Muhammad.

**'asharah mubashsharah** 'The ten who received good news.' Ten of the most distinguished Companions of the Prophet, who were promised entry to Paradise by the Prophet himself. They are
1) Abu Bakr,
2) 'Umar,
3) 'Uthman,
4) 'Ali,
5) Talhah,
6) Zubayr,
7) 'Abd ar-Rahman,
8) Sa'd ibn Abu Waqqas,
9) Sa'id ibn Zayd and
10) 'Ubaydah ibn al-Jarrah.

**'Ashura** The tenth day of the Muslim month of *Muharram*. The Prophet used to fast on this day and so it is still regarded as a holy day.

**Asiyah** The wife of Fir'awn. She ranks among the Four Perfect Women. [See also: ASHAB AL-KISA']

**al-Asma' al-Husna** 'The Most Beautiful Names.' This refers to the ninety-nine most beautiful names of Allah.

**'Asr** The afternoon prayer.

**Al-Aws** A major Arab tribe of Madinah which constituted an important section of the Ansar after the arrival of the Prophet in Madinah.

**ayah** Verse, especially a verse of the Qur'an. The word has the additional meaning of 'sign'.

**ayat al-Kursi** 'The Verse of the Throne.' The 253rd verse of *surah al-Baqarah*, which is one of the most famous and beloved verses of the Qur'an. It is frequently recited as a protection against evil.

**Ayyub (Job)** One of the prophets who was severely afflicted by Allah to test his loyalty for Him. Having passed the test, he was bestowed to his former state of well being. He is famous for his patience.

**Azar** Father of the Prophet Ibrahim. He was a pagan and a very determined idolator.

# B

**Badr, Battle of** The first major battle fought by the Prophet Muhammad with the support of the Madinans, against the Makkans at Badr.

**Bahira** Name of a Christian monk and hermit encountered by the Prophet while on a trading expedition to Syria when the Prophet was just about twelve years old. Bahira perceived by various signs that the young Muhammad would become a prophet and forecast great things for him.

**Banu Hilal** Najd based Arab tribe, some of whose members later migrated to Egypt.

**Banu Isra'il** "The Children of Israel." The Jews are

# a b c d e f g h i j k l m n o p q r s t u v w x y z

called the *Banu Isra'il* in the Qur'an.

**Banu Nadir** One of three major Jewish clans of Madinah during the time of *hijrah*.

**Banu Qurayzah** Major Jewish clan in Madinah accused by the Prophet of treachery after the siege and Battle of Khandaq.

**barakah** Blessing.

**barzakh** Obstacle, hindrance, barrier, partition. In Islam the word came to indicate an intermediate area between Hell and Heaven, as the place between this earthly life and the Hereafter.

**Basmala** *Bismillah al-Rahman al-Rahim*, meaning 'In the name of Allah, the Merciful, the Compassionate,' is an invocation frequently used at the commencement of any undertaking.

**Batin** Esoteric, inner.

**Bayt al-Haram** The Sacred House. One of the names of the Ka'bah.

**Bayt Allah** The House of Allah. Yet another name of the Ka'bah.

**Bayt al-Mal** The House of Property. The public treasury of a Muslim state, which the ruler is not allowed to use for his personal expenses, it being intended only for the public welfare.

**al-Bayt al-Ma'mur** 'The Inhabited House.' A house in the seventh heaven, visited by the Prophet during the *mi'raj*.

**Bayt al-Muqaddas** The Sacred House. A name given to the al-Aqsa mosque of Jerusalem.

**Bid'ah** Innovation, especially bad or hostile to Islamic law.

**Bilal ibn Rabah** An Abyssinian slave freed by Abu Bakr. He was the first *mu'adhdhin* appointed by the Prophet, and he served the Prophet in various other ways.

**Bilqis** Name of the Queen of Saba (Sheba), who was the contemporary of the Prophet Sulayman (Solomon). When the Prophet Sulayman invited her to accept the faith of the one true Allah, she immediately did so.

**Al-Bukhari** Very famous compiler of *Hadith* entitled *Sahih*, which contains about 600,000 traditions. His full name was Abu Abdullah Muhammad ibn Isma'il al-Bukhari and he was born at Bukhara.

**al-Buraq** The name of the animal, which the Prophet Muhammad mounted, in the company of the angel Jibril (Gabriel) to make his famous *isra'*, or night journey.

**burqa** Long veil for women which covers most of the body, except for the eyes.

# C

**Cain and Abel** [See: QABIL AND HABIL]

**caliph** [See: KHALIFAH]

**Camel, Battle of the** The battle fought near Basra between 'A'ishah, Talhah ibn Ubaydullah al-Taymi

# a b c **d e f** g h i j k l m n o p q r s t u v w x y z

and al-Zubayr ibn al-'Awwam on the one hand, and the forces of 'Ali ibn Abi Talib on the other. The battle was won by 'Ali.

**chadar** Large black cloak and veil which envelopes the entire body of a woman.

# D E F

**Al-Dajjal** 'The Cheater' or 'Antichrist.' A large number of traditions indicate that he will arrive on earth during the last days, that he will commit evil against the Muslims and will eventually be slain by the Prophet 'Isa, who will descend from Heaven. He is also called Masih ad-Dajjal.

**da'wah** Call to Islam or invitation to accept the faith of Allah. It is the duty of every Muslim man, woman and child to communicate the message of Islam to non-Muslims.

**Dawud** One of the prophets mentioned in the Qur'an. He was endowed with special gifts of justice and wisdom. He is also the recipient of the book of revelation called *Zabur* or Psalms.

**dhikr** 'Remembrance' in which the name of Allah or a phrase like *'Allahu Akbar'* or *'La ilaha illallah'*, is repeated over

a b c **d e f** g h i j k l m n o p q r s t u v w x y z

and over again in either a high or low voice, often linked with bodily movement or breathing.

**Dhu al-Kifl** Name of one of the prophets mentioned in the Qur'an.

**Dhu al-Qarnayn** 'He with the two horns.' This is the name of an important figure mentioned in the Qur'an who was endowed by Allah with earthly powers to punish wickedness and reward goodness. He travelled to the West and East and built a barrier to protect people against Yajuj and Majuj (Gog and Magog).

**dikka** (also **dakka**) Raised platform in a mosque, often positioned near the Minbar. On Friday at the congregational prayer, the *muadhdhin* uses the *dikka* to give the final call to prayer.

**din** Faith, religion, especially spiritual.

**diyyah** Blood money or compensation given by injurer or murderer to the victim or his family.

**Elephant, the Year of the** The year of 570 AD in which Abrahah made an unsuccessful attack on the city of Makkah. The year is so-called because there were one or more elephants in Abrahah's army.

**fada'il** Excellent qualities, merits, virtues.

**faqih** Jurist, jurisprudent. One who practises *fiqh*.

**fard** Religious duty that is incumbent upon Muslims.

**Fatimah** The daughter of the Prophet Muhammad and Khadijah. Fatimah was married to 'Ali and was the mother of Hasan and Husayn. She was very fond of her father and has been most respected and revered by the Muslims. She survived only six months after her father's death. 'She ranks among the *ashab al-kisa'*.

**Fatimids** Major dynasty in medieval Islamic history which flourished in North Africa and later in Egypt. It derived its name from Fatimah, the daughter of the Prophet.

**fatwa** A religious or judicial sentence pronounced by the *khalifah* or by a *mufti*, or a *qazi*.

**fidyah** An expiation for sin or for duties left undone.

**fiqh** Islamic jurisprudence.

**Fir'awn (Pharaoh)** The arrogant and wicked king of Egypt in the time of the Prophet Musa or Moses. His people were drowned in the waters of the Nile.

**Five Pillars of Islam** See [PILLARS OF ISLAM]

# G H

**ghusl** Major ritual washing of the whole body to achieve a state of purity and cleanliness.

**Gog and Magog** Yajuj and Majuj. They were a barbarous people of Central Asia, as mentioned in the Qur'an. They were said to spread evil in the lands of Dhu al-Qarnayn. He therefore built a barrier of iron and molten brass across

## a b c d e f g h i j k l m n o p q r s t u v w x y z

a mountain pass through which they used to come and attack his people.

**hadd** Boundary, limit.

**hadith** (pl. *ahadith*) Speech, report, narrative. A record of the sayings and actions of the Prophet Muhammad and his Companions, and as such is regarded by the Muslims as a source of Islamic law and ritual. Also called tradition.

**hadith qudsi** A sacred, or holy tradition. This is the name given to a tradition that records Allah's own utterances as opposed to those of the Prophet.

**Hafsa bint 'Umar** One of the wives of the Prophet Muhammad and daughter of 'Umar. She is particularly important in the traditional history of the Qur'an during the caliphate of 'Uthman.

**al-hajar al-aswad** 'The Black Stone,' set in the Ka'bah; those pilgrims near enough to it, will attempt to kiss the Black Stone during their circumambulation (*tawaf*) of the Ka'bah during the *hajj*.

**hajj** The pilgrimage to Makkah performed in the month of Dhu al-Hijja. *Hajj* is one of the five pillars of Islam.

**hajj al-wada'** 'The Pilgrimage of Farewell,' undertaken and led by the Prophet himself to Makkah, which became a model for future pilgrimages.

**halal** That which is permitted or lawful in Islam.

**Halimah bint Abu Dhu'ayb** Foster mother and wet-nurse of the Prophet Muhammad for his first two years of life. She belonged to the Banu Sa'd, a branch of the Hawazin tribe.

**al-hamdu lillah** A very commonly used invocation meaning 'Praise be to Allah.'

**hammam** Bathing place

**Hamza ibn 'Abd al-Muttalib** Paternal uncle of the Prophet Muhammad. At first he opposed Islam, but later became a valiant admirer of Islam. He fought bravely at the Battle of Badr and was martyred at the Battle of Uhud.

**hanif** Monotheist.

**haram** Sanctuary, an area of a particularly sacred nature, like Makkah and Madinah both of which are forbidden to non-Muslims because of their sacredness.

**al-haram al-sharif** 'The Noble Sanctuary.' Situated in the temple area of Jerusalem, it includes *al-Aqsa* mosque and the *Qubbat as-Sakhra*.

**al-haramayn** The Two Sacred Sanctuaries, i.e. the great mosque at Makkah and the Prophet's mosque at Madinah. [See also: THALITH AL-HARAMAYN]

**Harun al-Rashid** The fifth and perhaps most famous caliph of the 'Abbasid dynasty.

**Harun ibn 'Imran (Aaron)** Brother of the Prophet Musa who himself was a prophet. He helped in the mission of the Prophet Musa.

**hasan** Fair or good.

**al-Hasan ibn 'Ali** Son of 'Ali and Fatimah, and grandson of the Prophet Muhammad. He abdicated the caliphate in favour of Mu'awiyah ibn Abu Sufyan.

**Hashim** (1) Great-grandfather of the Prophet Muhammad whose name was borne by the Prophet's own clan. Hashim was son

## a b c d e f g **h** i j k l m n o p q r s t u v w x y z

of 'Abd Manaf and also father of 'Abd al-Muttalib.
(2) Makkan clan to which the Prophet belonged; it was a part of the Quraysh tribe.

**Hattin, Battle of** This was one of the great battles fought in an area north west of Lake Tiberias between the Christian Crusaders and Salah al-Din's army. The Christian forces, which included Raymond of Tripoli and Reginald of Kerak, were decisively beaten. This battle opened the way for the Muslim capture of Jerusalem.

**hawd** A pool, generally in a mosque, from which perform ritual ablution.

**al-Hawiya** One of the seven layers of Hell in which hypocrites will be punished.

**Hawwa' (Eve)** Wife of Adam, mother of mankind. She was tempted by *Shaytan* in Paradise and as a result, ate the forbidden fruit along with Adam. This incurred Allah's wrath and they were asked to leave Paradise.

**hijab** A veil worn by Muslim women in order to cover the body.

**al-hijrah** The Migration. This refers to the migration of the Prophet Muhammad from Makkah to Madinah in 622 AD.

**hilal** The new moon. A term used for the first three days of the month in the Islamic calendar.

**Hind** Wife of Abu Sufyan. At her instigation, one of her slaves killed Hamza at the Battle of Uhud.

**Hira** Cave situated to the north east of Makkah on the Mountain of Light, where the Prophet received the first revelation of the Qur'an through the angel Jibril (Gabriel).

a b c d e f g h **i** j k l m n o p q r s t u v w x y z

**Hud** A prophet sent to the people of 'Ad who rejected him and were subsequently destroyed by Allah.

**al-Hudaybiyyah, Treaty of** Major treaty concluded between the Makkans and the Prophet Muhammad in which the Prophet agreed to all the demands, of the Makkans so that peace might prevail in this region.

**hudhud (hoopoe)** The name of the bird which carried the letter from King Sulayman (Solomon) to the Queen of Saba (Sheba).

**hur** Female companions of the people of Paradise.

**Al-Husayn** Second son of 'Ali and Fatimah and grandson of the Prophet Muhammad. He was martyred at the Battle of Karbalah.

**Al-Hutamah** One of the seven layers of Hell to which Jews are assigned to be punished.

# I

**'ibadah** Worship

**Iblis** The Devil, also called Satan (*Shaytan*). In the Garden of Paradise, Iblis tempted Adam and Hawwa' and thus precipitated their downfall.

**Ibn 'Abbas** One of the Companions of the

a b c d e f g h **i** j k l m n o p q r s t u v w x y z

Prophet. His full name was 'Abdullah Ibn 'Abbas. He was also a cousin of the Prophet Muhammad. He is renowned as *Tarjumanul Qur'an* or "the interpreter of the Qur'an."

**Ibn Majah** One of the six principal compilers of Hadith. His compilation was named *Kitab al-Sunan*.

**Ibn Mas'ud** Notable Companion of the Prophet and a very early convert to Islam.

**Ibrahim** (1) A great Islamic prophet and ardent proponent of monotheism who figures prominently in the Qur'an. (2) Son of the Prophet Muhammad and Mariya the Copt. He died in infancy.

**'Id** Feast or festival.

**'Id al-adha** The Feast of Sacrifice. It is celebrated on the 10th day of the month of *Dhu al-Hijja*.

**'Id al-fitr** The Feast of Breaking the Fast of *Ramadan*. It is celebrated on the first day of the month of *Shawwal*.

**Idris** Name of a prophet mentioned in the Qur'an.

**iftar** The meal taken for breaking the fast after sunset during *Ramadan*.

**ihram** Ritual dress for the pilgrims during *hajj*. It consists of two new white cotton cloths, each six feet long by three and a half feet broad. One of these is called *rida'* and the other *izar*.

**i'jaz** Inimitability of the Qur'an. The sacred text challenges those who oppose it to produce its equal.

**ilhad** Heresy, a deviation from the correct path.

**'ilm** Knowledge.

**Ilyas** One of the prophets mentioned in the Qur'an.

**a b c d e f g h i j k l m n o p q r s t u v w x y z**

**imam** One who leads the prayer.

**iman** Faith.

**Al-Injil** The Gospel. The book that was revealed to the Prophet 'Isa, which later on became corrupted.

**insha Allah** 'If Allah wills.' A very common expression of Muslims. One should not talk about a future plan or occasion without adding *insha Allah*.

**Iram of the Pillars** A terrestrial paradise built by Shaddad in the desert of 'Adan, to rival the celestial one, and to be called Iram. On going to take possession of it, Shaddad and all his people were struck dead by a noise from heaven, and the man-made paradise disappeared.

**'Isa' (Jesus)** Son of Maryam (Mary). He was a major prophet with a prominent place in the Qur'an. Islam regards the Prophet 'Isa' as purely human and not as the son of God.

**Ishaq (Isaac)** Son of the Prophet Ibrahim and younger brother of Ishma'il (Ishmael).

**isharat al-sa'ah** The Signs of the Hour or of the Last Day. There are a large number of signs given both in the Qur'an and the Hadith about the Last Day.

**Islam** The religion preached by the Prophet Muhammad. The word 'Islam' literally means 'submission' (to the will of Allah).

**Isma'il (Ishmael)** Name of one of the prophets. Son of the Prophet Ibrahim and Hajar. Together with his father he rebuilt the Ka'bah.

**isnad** Chain of authorities establishing the veracity of a *hadith*.

a b c d e f g h i **j** k l m n o p q r s t u v w x y z

**Isra'** Night Journey. The most famous night journey made by the Prophet Muhammad. Mounted on his steed, al-Buraq, he flew through the air from Makkah to Jerusalem and from there ascended to heaven.

**Israfil** Name of one of the angels who will blow the trumpet on the Day of Resurrection.

**i'tikaf** Seeking retirement in a mosque during the last ten days of *Ramadan*, during which time the worshipper does not leave the mosque, except for necessary purposes.

**'Izra'il** The Angel of Death, or *Malak al-Mawt*. He comes to a man at the hour of death to carry his soul away from the body.

# J

**Jahannam** This is the name of one of the seven layers of Hell, in which the unrepentant, wicked Muslims would be punished.

**jahiliyah** State of ignorance. The word designates the pre-Islamic period.

**al-Jahim** Name of one of the seven layers of Hell to which idolators are assigned to be punished.

**al-Jamra** The Pebble. Three stone pillars in the valley of Mina, each called a *jamra*, are visited by the pilgrims

a b c d e f g h i **j** k l m n o p q r s t u v w x y z

returning from 'Arafat during the *hajj*. The pilgrims throw tiny pebbles at them to show symbolically how believers should avoid Satan's temptations.

**Janazah** A funeral prayer performed for the recently deceased.

**al-Jannah** The Garden. The most common name by which Paradise is referred to in the Qur'an.

**Jerusalem** In Arabic this major city is called *al-Quds*, which means 'The Holy.' Jerusalem is revered as the third holiest city in Islam, after Makkah and Madinah since it is the site from which the Prophet made his famous *mi'raj*, through the seven heavens.

**Jibril** Arabic name of the Angel Gabriel. He is one of the greatest angels and it was through him that the Holy Qur'an was revealed by Allah to the Prophet.

**jihad** An effort, or striving, especially for the cause of Islam.

**jinn** Intelligent, often invisible beings made from fire (by contrast with the angels, made from light and with mankind, made from clay). They also have the ability to assume various kinds of perceptible forms.

**jizya** Poll tax imposed in medieval times on non-Muslims who were "people of the Book" (*Ahl al-Kitab*) in areas ruled by Muslims.

# K

**Ka'bah** A cube shaped building within the precincts of the Great Mosque of Makkah. The Prophet Ibrahim and his son Isma'il are revered as rebuilders of the Ka'bah, originally established by Adam. However, it is most important to note that Muslims do not worship the Ka'bah, nor the Black Stone (*Hajar al-Aswad*) set into one of its corners. The Ka'bah is an ancient sanctuary designed to insplore man to worship Allah.

**kafir** Unbeliever, infidel.

**kafur** Camphor. A cup of *kafur*, sometimes identified by tradition as a fountain in Paradise, will be drunk by the pious.

**Karbalah** Central Iraqi city with a domed sepulchre containing the body of Husayn ibn 'Ali, who was martyred at a battle fought there.

**Khadijah bint Khuwaylid** First wife of the Prophet Muhammad and revered as the first Muslim after him. She ranks among the *ashab al-kisa'* (Four Perfect women).

**Khalid ibn Walid** Belonged to the Makhzum clan of the Quraysh tribe. Having fought against the Prophet Muhammad at the Battle of Uhud, he

**a b c d e f g h i j k l m n o p q r s t u v w x y z**

later converted to Islam and became one of its noted generals. Khalid fought at the battles of Aqraba, Ajnadayn and Yarmuk, among others.

**khalifah** Caliph. Head of the Islamic Community.

**al-Khalil** The Friend. The Prophet Ibrahim bears the title 'The Friend of Allah' or *Khalilullah*.

**khamr** Wine. Drinking of wine is prohibited in Islam.

**Al-Khandaq, Siege** The word *khandaq* means a trench. This battle was the third major confrontation between the Prophet, after his emigration to Madinah, and the Makkans. To protect the Madinans from the onslaught of the Makkans, the Prophet, on the advice of Salman Farisi, had a trench dug to the north of the oasis. Several assaults over a period of about two weeks were successfully checked by the trench.

**kharaj** Land tax.

**Khatam an-Nabiyyun** The Seal of the Prophets. A title given to the Prophet Muhammad in the Qur'an.

**khayrat** Charity, almsgiving.

**Khubayb** One of the early martyrs of Islam. Whilst being tortured at the stake, he was asked whether he did not wish the Prophet was in his place. He replied "I would not wish to be with my family, my possession and my children, even if the Prophet were only to be pricked with a thorn." When they had bound to the stake, his enemies said, "Now abjure Islam, and we'll let you go." He replied, "Not for the whole world."

**Khuld** Eternity.

**khutbah** Sermon, address. The sermon delivered before the Friday Prayer. *Khutbah* is also delivered during the prayers of *'Id al-fitr* and *'Id al-adha*.

**khutbatul-waqfah** Sermon of the rite Standing. The sermon preached on Mount Arafat at the midday prayer on the ninth day of *hajj*.

**kiram al-katibun** The Noble Writers. The two recording angels who are attached to every person: one at the right shoulder to record good deeds and the other at the left to record evil deeds.

**kiswah** Brocaded black cover of silk and cotton which covers the Ka'bah. It is replaced with a new one once a year.

**al-Kitab** The Book. The term generally refers to the Holy Qur'an.

**al-Kufah** A city on the west bank of the river Euphrates in Iraq. The mosque of 'Ali ibn Abi Talib, who was assassinated there, is still in existence. Kufi or Kufic script is named after Kufa, as this oldest style of Arabic writing originated in this city.

**Kufic Script** See: [AL-KUFAH]

**kufr** Infidelity, unbelief. Disbelieving in any of the tenets of Islam.

**kusuf** Eclipse.

# L

**Labid** The son of Rabi'ah ibn Ja'far al-'Amiri, a celebrated poet who lived in the days of the Prophet. He died at al-Kufah at the age of 157 years. The Prophet is reported to have said: "The truest words ever uttered by a poet are those of Labid—'Know that everything is vanity but Allah.'"

**lahd** The hollow made in a grave on the *qiblah* side, in which the dead body is placed. It is made the same length as the grave, and is as high as would allow a person to sit up in it.

**La ilaha illallah** The first part of *shahadah*, which means: "There is no diety but Allah."

**la'nah** Imprecation, curse.

**Lapwing** See: [HUDHUD]

**laqab** A surname—either a title of honour or a nickname.

**al-Lat** Name of a female idol which was worshipped by the Thaqif tribe in the pre-Islamic period.

**lawh al-mahfuz** The Preserved Tablet. This is a tablet in heaven inscribed with the original text of the Qur'an.

a b c d e f g h i j k **l** m n o p q r s t u v w x y z

**Laylatul Bara'ah** The 15th day of the month of *Sha'ban*, which is also called *Laylatu 'n-nisf min Sha'ban*, or "the night of the middle of *Sha'ban*." Also in Persian "*Shab-i-Barat*," which is the most popular among Muslims. Muslims keep awake the whole night, to repeat one hundred *rakah* prayers and fast the next day.

**Laylat-ul-Qadr** The Night of Power in which the Qur'an was revealed. The excellences of this night are said to be innumerable, and it is believed that, during its solemn hours, the whole of animate and inanimate creation bows down in humble adoration of Allah.

**Laylatul Mi'raj** The Night of Ascension (of The Prophet Muhammad). A popular festival celebrates this event on the 27th of *Rajab*, the seventh month of the Islamic year. In some Asian countries it is known as *Shab-i-Mi'raj*.

**Laza** Blazing fire. Laza is the name of one of the seven layers of Hell.

**libas** Dress.

**locusts** Locusts are lawful food for Muslims without being killed by *zabah*.

**Luqman** Known as Luqman al-Hakim or Luqman the Philosopher, he is mentioned in the Qur'an as one upon whom Allah had bestowed wisdom.

**Lut (Lot)** One of the prophets, who was sent by Allah to warn his people against crime. But the people denied him. As a result, Allah destroyed the whole city and all the people in it, except for Lut and his family. Lut's wife, however, perished because she lingered after the others had gone.

**Lying** The Prophet Muhammad is related to have said: "When a servant of Allah tells a lie, his guardian angels move a mile away from him because of its foul odour.

# M

**madhhab** Ideology, doctrine, creed or movement.

**al-Madinah** Literally, 'The City.' This is the second holiest city in Islam after Makkah. Its early name was Yathrib. It became famous after giving shelter to the Prophet Muhammad at the time of *hijrah*. It is here that the Prophet lies buried. The city is frequently characterised by the epithet 'The Radiant' (*al-Munawwarah*).

**madrasah** School, college (especially, for Islamic education).

**Madyan** The people of the Prophet Shuayb, who rejected him and received divine punishment.

**maghazi** Raids, military campaigns, expeditions, especially those undertaken by the Prophet Muhammad.

**al-Mahdi** Literally 'The Rightly Guided One.' A ruler who shall appear

a b c d e f g h i j k l **m** n o p q r s t u v w x y z

upon earth in the last days and will spread equity and justice all over the world.

**majlis** Meeting place, gathering, assembly.

**Makkah** The holiest city in Islam. Muslims turn towards Makkah in prayer and undertake *hajj* to this city, because of the Ka'bah being situated there. The Qur'an was first revealed near this city and it was from Makkah that the Prophet made his famous *hijrah* to Madinah. Makkah is often characterised as 'The Revered' (*al-Mukarramah*) and also referred to as 'The Mother of Cities'.

**makruh** That which is hateful and unbecoming.

**malak** [ANGEL]

**Malak al-Mawt** ['IZRA'IL]

**Malik** The angel who is the chief of the guardians of Hell.

**mamluk** A slave.

**Manaf** Name of an idol worshipped in the pre-Islamic period in ancient Arabia.

**manarah** Minaret. A minaret is the tower of a mosque from which the call to prayer is made.

**Manat** Name of an idol worshipped in the period of *jahiliyyah*.

**Maqam Ibrahim** "The Place of Ibrahim." A heavenly place mentioned in the Qur'an, which is reserved for the Prophet Ibrahim.

**Maqam Mahmud** "A Glorious Place." A place in heaven said to be reserved for the Prophet Muhammad.

**Mariyah al-Qibtiyah** One of the wives of the Prophet Muhammad, she was the mother of his son Ibrahim.

**Marwah** A hill near Makkah. For details see al-Safa.

**Maryam** The mother of the Prophet 'Isa', was the Daughter of 'Imran and his wife Hannah and the sister of Harun. She ranks among the *ashab al-kisa'*.

**al-Masih** Literally, 'The Messiah.' This is a title given to the Prophet 'Isa' in the Qur'an.

**Al-Masihu 'd-Dajjal** [AL-DAJJAL]

**masjid** Mosque. The word literally means 'a place of bowing down'. A mosque is generally built in the form of a square, in the centre of which is an open courtyard. The centre of the wall facing the Ka'bah is the *mihrab* and to the right of this is the *minbar* from which the *khutbah* is preached. It is impermissible to enter a mosque while in a state of impurity.

**al-Masjid al-Haram** The Great Mosque of Makkah. This is a major focal point for *hajj*.

**masnun** That which is founded upon the percept of the practice of the Prophet Muhammad.

**matn** The main text of a *hadith* as distinct from the *isnad*.

**mawdu'** In *hadith* criticism. This word has the technical sense of 'invented' when used to describe a *hadith*.

**mawt** Death. In other words, the departure of the soul from the body.

**Maymunah** One of the wives of Prophet Muhammad.

**mida'a** Ablution fountain, located in a mosque for ritual ablution before prayers. Considerable artistry often went into the design of the medieval *mida'a*; its modern counterpart is frequently wrought in a similarly beautiful fashion.

**mi'dhana** (also **ma'dhana**) Place from which the call to prayer is made, a minaret.

**mihrab** A niche within a mosque indicating the direction of the *qiblah* and before which the *imam* takes his position to lead the congregation in prayer.

**Mika'il** Name of one of the great Islamic angels who is responsible for bringing down the rain.

**Mina** A sacred valley near Makkah. An animal is sacrificed at Mina during the *hajj* as the climactic event of the *hajj*.

**minbar** The pulpit, close to the *mihrab*, from which the *khutbah* is delivered by the *imam*.

**miqat** Literally, 'meeting point.' The places at which Makkan pilgrims assume *ihram*. Five of these places were designated by the Prophet himself, and the sixth has since been added to suit the convenience of travellers from the East. They are as follows: (1) Dhu'l-Hulara' for the pilgrims of Madinah; (2) Juhfah, for Syria; (3) Qarnu'l-Manazil, for Najd; (4) Yawlamlam, for Yaman; (5) Dhat-i-'Irq, for Iraq and (6) Ibrahim Mursia, for those coming from India and the East.

**mi'raj** Ascension. The Prophet Muhammad's journey from Jerusalem through the Seven Heavens after the *isra'* from Makkah.

**miskin** A poor person.

**miswak** (1) A tooth cleaner made of the wood, of the *Salvadora Indica* tree. The stick is about nine inches in length. (2) The act of cleaning the teeth, as

a b c d e f g h i j k l **m** n o p q r s t u v w x y z

the (voluntary) first part of ablution.

**mizan** A balance.

**modesty** (Ar. *haya'*) According to the Prophet Muhammad, 'modesty is a branch of faith.'

**mu'adhdhin** The person who gives the call to prayer (*adhan*) from the minaret of a mosque.

**Mu'awiyah ibn Abu Sufyan** Governor of Syria and later, founder of the Umayyad dynasty. After the murder of 'Ali he became the *sixth khalifah*.

**al-mu'awwidhatan** Literally, 'the seekers of refuge.' The last two *surahs* of the Qur'an, namely; *al-Falaq* and *an-Nas* are together called as *al-mu'awwidhatan*, which are frequently recited as a protection from evil.

**mufti** One who delivers, or is qualified to deliver *fatwa*.

**muhaddith** (1) A narrator of a *hadith*. (2) One who has learned a vast number of *ahadith* (traditions).

**al-muhajirun** The Emigrants. The people who migrated from Makkah to Madinah at the time of *hijrah* and assisted the Prophet there.

**Muhammad** Muhammad, upon whom be peace, is the Prophet and Founder of Islam. He was the most significant and last ever Prophet sent by Allah. He was the son of 'Abd Allah and Aminah. He received the first revelation of the Qur'an from the angel Jibril when he was forty years old. Later, throughout his life, he preached Islam.

**mujahid** One who struggles for the cause of Islam.

**mujtahid** Literally, "one who strives" to attain a high position of scholarship and learning.

**mulhid** An infidel; one who has deviated or turned aside from the truth.

**mulla** A Persian form used for the Arabic *mawlawi*, "a learned man, a scholar."

**mu'min** One who believes in the fundamentals of Islam.

**munafiq** Hypocrite. One who outwardly professes to believe in Islam, but secretly denies the faith. The hypocrites will be in the lowest layer of Hell, unless they repent.

**munajat** Supplication. Generally by raising both palms, a personal supplication made before Allah after finishing the usual prayers (*salah*).

**munfiq** "One who spends." A charitable person.

**Munkar and Nakir** Names of two angels of the grave. These two angels play a significant role in the after-life of man. They visit the dead in their graves and interrogate them as to their belief in the Prophet and his religion.

**muqarnas** Term used in Islamic architecture to denote the honeycomb or hanging decoration which often appears within a mosque or mausoleum dome, or at the top of a *mihrab*, window or large door.

**muqtadi** Follower. The individual or group standing behind the *imam* in the ritual prayers.

**murid** A disciple of some *murshid*, or leader of a religious order.

a b c d e f g h i j k l **m** n o p q r s t u v w x y z

**mursal** A prophet or a messenger. A term for prophets used in the Qur'an.

**murshid** A guide. The title given to the spiritual director of a religious order.

**Musa (Moses)** He was a major prophet and messenger who proclaimed his mission in the presence of Firawn (Pharaoh). He was known as *kalimullah,* or 'one who conversed with Allah'. During his mission he was supported by his brother Harun, who himself was a Prophet.

**musalla** A small mat, cloth or carpet upon which Muslims say their prayers.

**mushrik** One who ascribes companions to Allah. An idolater.

**Muslim** One who professes and practises the faith of Islam.

**Muslim ibn al-Hajjaj, Abu 'l-Husayn** A very famous compiler of *Hadith*. His collection, called the *Sahih,* is almost as famous as that of al-Bukhari.

**mustahabb** The category of actions which, although not obligatory in Islamic law, are recommended.

**mu'tamir** A performer of the *'Umrah*.

**mutawwif** Pilgrim guide in Makkah whose function is to guide the visiting pilgrims through the rituals of *hajj*.

**Muzdalifa** A place near Makkah between 'Arafat and Mina. Pilgrims spend the night here after returning from 'Arafat.

# N

**nabi** Prophet. One sent by Allah to preach Allah's religion to mankind.

**Nafisa, al-Sayyida** Great-grand-daughter of al-Hasan ibn 'Ali. She migrated to Egypt and gained a reputation as a miracle worker. Her shrine is situated in Cairo.

**Namrud** He is a king identified with the figure who cast the Prophet Ibrahim into a blazing fire, which, however, became cold by Allah's decree.

**al-Nar** Literally, 'The Fire.' A common name for Hell.

**an-Nasa'i** Compiler of one of the six major compilations of *Hadith*.

**nasara** The Arabic name for the Christians.

**al-Nawawi** Name of a Syrian scholar from Nawa. He is most famous for his short collection of *Hadith*, known in English as *Forty Hadith*.

**nikah** Marriage.

**niyyah** Intention. Islamic moral theology and Islamic ritual, placing considerable emphasis on the intention of an individual.

**Nuh (Noah)** One of the prophets whom his people rejected. The people consequently drowned in a great flood, while Nuh was saved in an ark which he built at the behest of Allah.

# P

**Pillars of Islam** (Ar. *Arkan al-Islam*) Faith (*shahadah*), prayers (*salat*), fasting (*sawm*), almsgiving (*zakat*) and pilgrimage (Hajj).

**pride** (Ar. *kibr*) Pride is forbidden in Islam. The Qur'an says: "Walk not proudly on the earth; truly, you can by no means cleave the earth, neither can you reach the mountains in height: all this is evil to your Lord and odious."

# Q

**Qabil and Habil (Cain and Abel)** The two sons of the Prophet Adam. Qabil became the first murderer on the earth by killing his brother Habil, who was innocent.

**qabr** Grave. Muslim graves are dug so as to allow the dead body to lie with its face towards the Ka'bah. They are customarily dug to a depth which would bring an averaged-sized a b c d e f g h i j k l m n o p **q** r s t u v w x y z

gravedigger's chest level with the surface. A recess *lahd*, is made, at the bottom, in which the body is placed, after which it is closed in with unburnt bricks, the grave is filled with earth and a mound is raised over it.

**qari'** A reader. A term used for one who reads the Qur'an correctly, and is acquainted with the science of reading the Qur'an.

**qarz** Loan, especially without interest.

**al-Qasim** Son of the Prophet Muhammad who died in infancy.

**Qaynuqa'** Major Jewish clan in Madinah, during the time of the Prophet Muhammad.

**qiblah** Direction of prayer towards the Ka'bah at Makkah.

**Quba', Masjid of.** A mosque near Madinah, built by the Prophet after his flight from Makkah, at the place where his camel knelt down at the end of the journey.

**qubbah** Dome, cupola. This is a major architectural feature of Islamic mosques and shrines.

**Qubbat as-Sakhra** The Dome of the Rock. This is the principal Islamic shrine in Jerusalem built over the area of rock on the Temple Mount from which the Prophet made his famous *mi'raj*.

**Qur'an** Name of the Sacred Book of Islam, which was revealed to the Prophet Muhammad through angel Jibril. It contains Allah's own words in the Arabic language. The Qur'an consists of 114 chapters, each called a *surah*. *Surahs* are further divided into verses, called *ayah*. The Qur'an is also known as *Umm al-Kitab,* or the Mother of Books. It is the most revered and inimitable book for Muslims.

**Quraysh** A major Arabian tribe in Makkah from which the Prophet Muhammad was descended and of which his grandfather 'Abd al-Muttalib was the chief. This tribe occupies a very prominent place in the Qur'an and in Islamic history. The *Hadith* has a special section set apart for a record of the sayings of the Prophet regarding the good qualities of this tribe.

# R

**rahil** A small book stand which can be folded up for convenience.

**al-Rajim** An epithet applied to Iblis or Shaytan (Satan) which means 'The Outcast.'

**Ramadan** The month of fasting which falls in the ninth month of the Muslim calendar. Fasting throughout Ramadan is one of the five pillars of Islam.

**Rashidun** A title applied to each of the first four 'Rightly Guided Caliphs' (*al-Khulafa' al-Rashidun*) who led the Islamic Community in its early days after the death of the Prophet Muhammad.

**rasul** A messenger or prophet.

**riba** Usury. The charging of interest on a loan. This is forbidden in Islam.

**Ridwan** Name of the angel in charge of Jannah.

**rizq** Sustenance.

**ruh** Soul, spirit.

**ruku'** A posture adopted in the daily prayers. The head is bowed and the palms of the hands rest on the knees.

**Ruqayyah** Name of one of the daughters of the Prophet Muhammad.

# S

**sabr** Patience. Patience is one of the virtues most emphasized in the Qur'an.

**sadaqah** Almsgiving

**as-Safa** Small hill now enclosed within the Great Mosque at Makkah. It is 1247 feet from another similarly enclosed hill called al-Marwah. During the *hajj* and *'umrah*, the ritual of the *sa'y* takes place between these two small hills. This ritual of *sa'y* is undertaken following the *tawaf* of the Ka'bah during the *hajj*.

**saff** An even row or line of things. A term used for a row of persons standing up for prayers.

a b c d e f g h i j k l m n o p q r **s** t u v w x y z

**al-Saffah** First ruler of the dynasty of the Abbasids which succeeded the Umayyads.

**Safiyah bint Huyayy** One of the wives of the Prophet Muhammad.

**safiyullah** 'The Chosen one of Allah.' A title given to the Prophet Adam.

**sahaba** Companions of the Prophet Muhammad.

**sahih** Technical term in *Hadith,* indicating the highest level of authenticity and trustworthiness in a tradition.

**sahm** Dish, yard, courtyard. In Islamic architecture this word is used specifically for a mosque's central courtyard.

**suhur** The meal which is taken before dawn during the fasting of Ramadan.

**Sa'ir** One of the seven ranks of Hell.

**salah** The Prayer. There are five daily prayers which are established by divine commandment for Muslims. These are: (1) *salatul fajr* or the prayer of dawn, (2) *salatul zuhr* or the midday prayer, (3) *salatul 'asr* or the afternoon prayer, (4) *salatul maghrib* or the evening prayer and (5) *salatul 'isha'* or the night prayer. Besides these five daily prayers there are various other prayers, some of which are non-obligatory.

**Salah al-Din** He is one of the great heroes of Islamic history, esteemed also in the West, because of his interaction with King Richard the Lionheart of England. He is justly famed for defeating of the Crusaders at the Battle of Hattin and the subsequent conquest of Jerusalem.

**as-salamu 'alaykum** "Peace be upon you." The common salutation among Muslims.

**salatul hajah** The prayer of necessity.

**salatul 'idayn** Prayers of the two festivals, namely, 'Id ul-Fitr and 'Id ul-Adha.

**salatul istikharah** A prayer seeking guidance.

**salatul janazah** The funeral prayer.

**salatul Jumu'ah** The prayer of assembly or the Friday prayer.

**salatul khawf** The prayer of fear.

**salatul khusuf** Prayers said during an eclipse of the moon.

**salatul kusuf** Prayers said during an eclipse of the sun.

**salatul mariz** The prayer said by the sick. When a person is too sick to stand up for the usual prayers, he is allowed to recite them either in a reclining or sitting posture, provided he performs the usual ablutions. It is ruled that he shall in such a case make the prostrations, etc., mentally.

**salatun nafl** Optional prayer.

**salatur ragha'ib** The prayer for things desired.

**salatus safar** The prayer of travel. A shortened recital of prayer allowed to travellers.

**salatut tarawih** The prayer of rest. Prayers recited after the night prayer during the month of Ramadan.

**salatul tasbih** The prayer of praise.

**Salih** The name of a prophet sent to warn

the people of Thamud, who not only rejected Salih's message but who also hamstrung the she-camel which was sent as a 'proof' and a 'sign' from Allah. The Thamud people were consequently destroyed in an earthquake.

**Salman al-Farisi** Early convert to Islam and a Companion of the Prophet Muhammad, who suggested the digging of a trench before the Siege and Battle of al-Khandaq.

**Salsabil** Name of a fountain in Paradise.

**Saqar** Name of one of the seven layers of Hell.

**saqim** Literally, sick, infirm. This is a technical term used in Hadith criticism to indicate the lowest acceptable level of trustworthiness in a tradition.

**Sawdah bint Zam'a** A wife of the Prophet Muhammad and a member of the Quraysh tribe. She married the Prophet after being widowed. Her first husband was al-Sakran ibn 'Amr, who was an early convert to Islam.

**sawm** Fasting, one of the five pillars of Islam.

**sa'y** Running between Safa and Marwah during *hajj*.

**shahadah** Bearing witness (to faith). This is one of the five pillars of Islam.

**shahid** Martyr. Islam assures believers that those who die as martyrs in battle, fighting in defence of their faith, will go to Paradise.

**shari'ah** Islamic law.

**Shi'ah** Those who follow and accept the claims of 'Ali ibn Abi Talib.

**shirk** Polytheism. Associating anything or

anyone with Allah. This is an unpar-donable sin and hence strictly forbidden in Islam.

**Shu'ayb** Arabian prophet sent to warn the people of Madyan to worship the one true Allah and to give up sharp business practices; they rejected his message and were punished accordingly in an earthquake.

**as-siddiq** The Righteous, the Honest, the Truthful One. A title borne both by Abu Bakr and the Prophet Yusuf.

**sidrat al-muntaha** The Furthest Lote Tree, in the seventh heaven, having its roots in the sixth. Its fruits are like water pots, and its leaves are like elephants' ears.

**Sirat al-Jahim** The bridge of Hell.

**Sirat al-Mustaqim** The straight path.

**slaughter, ritual** Animals for human consumption by Muslims should be ritually slaughtered. Components of this ritual include the recitation of the phrase 'In the name of Allah; Allah is Most Great' over the animal and the draining off of as much blood as possible. The slaughterer should be a Muslim himself.

**subhah** Rosary. A full Islamic rosary comprises 99 beads, each indicating one of the 99 beautiful names of Allah. There are also rosaries of 33 beads.

**sufi** Islamic mystic.

**Sulayman (Solomon)** He was a prophet and king, distinguished by his wisdom and arcane knowledge. He was acquainted with the language of the birds and insects.

**Sumayya bint Khubbat** A woman highly revered

as Islam's first martyr; she was killed by Abu Jahl.

**sunnah** A path or way; a manner of life. It developed from the meaning of 'customary practice' to indicating the specific actions and sayings of the Prophet Muhammad.

**Sunni** One who adheres to the sunnah or customary practice of the Prophet Muhammad.

**surah** Chapter of the Qur'an. Each chapter is divided into a number of verses, or *ayat*.

# T

**tabi'un** Followers; the next generation after the *sahabah*, or companions.

**Tabuk** Town in the northern Arabian peninsula, near the Gulf of al-'Aqaba, to which the Prophet Muhammad led his greatest expedition.

**tafsir** Commentary, especially relating to the Qur'an.

**taharah** Ritual purification or cleanliness. Islam places great stress on the concepts of inner and outer purity.

**at-Ta'if** Town, about forty miles from Makkah, whose people stoned the Prophet during his early attempts to establish contact with him. On the way back to Makkah, one night after his visit to at-Tai'f, the Prophet gave the message of the Qur'an to a company of jinn.

**takbir** Praise, glorification, the declaration or expression: 'Allah is Most Great' (Allahu Akbar).

**Talhah b. 'Ubaydullah al-Taymi** A very early convert to Islam and Companion of the Prophet Muhammad.

**tasbih** Glorification, praising of Allah, i.e. by saying the phrase *Subhan-Allah* which means 'Praise be to Allah.'

**Tasnim** Name of a fountain in Paradise.

**tawaf** Circumambulation of the Ka'bah seven times at the beginning of *hajj*.

**tawaf al-wada'** At the end of *hajj*, before departing from Makkah 'the circumambulation of farewell,' may be performed but it is not compulsory.

**tawbah** Repentance. To be very sorry about a misdeed and to promise never to commit it again. Those who turn to Allah in repentance will be forgiven.

**tawhid** Declaration of the Oneness of Allah. This is one of the most fundamental doctrines of Islam.

**Tawrah (Torah)** The divine book that was revealed to the Prophet Musa (Moses).

**tayammum** The substitution for *wudu*, performed with sand, in case water is not available or the person is so sick that the use of water would be harmful to his health.

**Thalith al-Haramayn** 'The Third Sacred Sanctuary.' The al-Aqsa mosque of Jerusalem is called by this name. The other two sacred sanctuaries are situated at Makkah and Madinah.

**Thamud** An arrogant tribe of the pre-Islamic era, to whom Allah had sent the Prophet Salih. They not only rejected the message of the Prophet Salih, but they hamstrung the she-camel which was sent as a 'proof' and 'sign' from Allah. Allah's wrath descended upon them and they were destroyed by a violent earthquake.

**tilawah** Recitation of the Qur'an.

**al-Tirmidhi, Abu 'Isa Muhammad** One of the six major compilers of Hadith.

**tradition** A record of the sayings and deeds of the Prophet Muhammad, which is called 'Hadith' in Arabic.

# U

**Uhud, Battle of** Second major battle fought between the Prophet Muhammad and the Makkans.

**'ulama'** Religious scholars, learned men.

**'Umar ibn al-Khattab** The second caliph and a very close Companion of the Prophet Muhammad. His daughter Hafsah was a wife of the Prophet. He was assassinated by a Persian slave, named Firoz.

**Umayyads** First major dynasty in medieval Islamic history, which

## a b c d e f g h i j k l m n o p q r s t **u** v w x y z

established itself in Damascus after the death of 'Ali ibn Abi Talib.

**ummah** Community, people.

**Umm Habibah** Widowed daughter of Abu Sufyan, who later married the Prophet Muhammad.

**Ummi** Illiterate, unlettered. The Prophet Muhammad is described as *Nabi al-Ummi*: the phrase is usually translated as 'the unlettered Prophet.'

**Umm Kulthum** Daughter of the Prophet Muhammad from his wife Khadijah. Umm Kulthum married 'Uthman ibn 'Affan. She died at the time of the expedition to Tabuk.

**Umm al-Kitab** Mother of the Book. The Qur'an is known as the "Mother of the Books". [See also: QUR'AN]

**Umm al-Mu'minin** "Mother of the Faithful." The wives of the Prophet Muhammad are revered as Mothers of the Faithful.

**Umm al-Qura** "Mother of the Villages." A name given to Makkah.

**Umm Salamah** Widow of Abu Salamah, who later married the Prophet Muhammad. She belonged to the Makhzum clan of the Quraysh tribe.

**'Umrah** A minor pilgrimage with the ceremonies of circumambulation of the Ka'bah, and running between Safa and Marwah, but omitting the sacrifices, etc.

**'Uthman ibn 'Affan** The third *khalifah* who came to power after the death of 'Umar ibn al-Khattab.

**al-'Uzza** The name of an idol that was worshipped in the pre-Islamic period.

# W X Y Z

**wali** Saint, holy man.

**Waraqah ibn Nawfal** He was a Christian and cousin of Khadijah, to whom she first confided about the revelation which came down to the Prophet Muhammad during his period of seclusion at Mount Hira'. Waraqah confirmed it to be true and assured her about the prophethood of the Prophet Muhammad.

**wudu'** Ablution or minor ritual washing of parts of one's body before the observance of a rite.

**wuquf** Standing at 'Arafah as one of the rites of hajj.

**yahud** Arabic name for the tribe of Jews.

**Yahya** (John) Son of Zakariyyah. He was also a prophet.

**Ya'qub (Jacob)** Name of a prophet mentioned in the Qur'an. He was the father of the Prophet Yusuf and the son of the Prophet Ishaq.

**Yathrib** The old name of Madinah.

**yawm al-akhir** The Last Day.

**yawm al-'ashura'** The tenth day of the month of Muharram.

**yawm al-Jumu'ah** The Day of Congregation—Friday. Friday is an important day for

**a b c d e f g h i j k l m n o p q r s t u v w x y z**

Muslims. Muslims gather in the mosque on this day to perform the congregational Friday prayer.

**yawm al-Qayamah** Day of Resurrection.

**Yunus (Jonah)** Name of a prophet. He was swallowed by a big fish and later released by supplicating to Allah. This supplication is known as du'a-i-Yunus. It is recited at times of distress.

**Yusuf (Joseph)** Name of a prophet who was the son of the Prophet Ya'qub. He was endowed with the knowledge of interpreting dreams. His jealous brothers threw him into a dry well. Afterwards a caravan took him to Egypt, where he received a higher position in the King's palace for his ability to interpret dreams.

**al-Zabaniyyah** The principal guardian angels of Hell.

**zabh** The ritual slaughter of an animal to make its flesh lawful for food. This is done by cutting the throat of the animal while reciting 'Bismillah Allahu Akbar', i.e. 'In the name of Allah, Allah is Most Great', and draining off as much blood as possible. The slaughterer should be a Muslim. The meat of such animals which are not which slain by the method of *zabh*, is unlawful and forbidden to Muslims.

**Zabur** Arabic name of the book of Psalms which was revealed to the Prophet Dawud, or David.

**zakah** Obligatory alms-tax which is one of the five pillars of Islam.

**Zakariyyah** Father of the Prophet Yahya.

**a b c d e f g h i j k l m n o p q r s t u v w x y z**

**Zamzam, Well of** A sacred well within the precincts of the Ka'bah. This well was shown by the angel Jibril to Hajar, which saved her son Isma'il's life. Muslims on *hajj* usually drink from this well, and take water as a souvenir. The water of Zamzam is considered to be of great sacredness and to have great healing powers.

**al-zaqqum** Bitter smelling and fearsome tree in the pit of Hell with flowers which resemble demonic heads.

**Zayd ibn Harith** Originally a slave of Khadijah, but later freed and adopted by the Prophet Muhammad.

**Zaynab bint Muhammad** Daughter of the Prophet Muhammad.

**zuhra** A title given to the Prophet's daughter Fatimah.

# Life of the Prophet Muhammad ﷺ

The Prophet Muhammad ﷺ was born in 570 A.D. in Makkah, Saudi Arabia. His father's name was Abdullah and his mother's name was Aminah. The Prophet Muhammad's father died two months before his birth. Following the old Arabian custom, the little Muhammad ﷺ was sent to spend the first years of his life with a wet nurse. His foster mother, whose name was Halimah, lived in a desert near Makkah.

When Muhammad ﷺ was six years old, his mother took him to visit his uncles in Yathrib, a place now known as Madinah. It was a long journey by caravan, but young Muhammad ﷺ enjoyed meeting his cousins, playing with them and learning to swim. But, tragically, on the journey back to Makkah, Aminah fell ill and died. Muhammad ﷺ returned home with his mother's maid, Barakah. As Muhammad ﷺ grew up, he was looked after by his grandfather, Abd al-Muttalib, and later by his uncle, Abu Talib.

When Muhammad ﷺ was about 12 years old, his uncle took him to Syria on a trade visit. It was a trip full of adventures. By the time he was 25 years old, Muhammad ﷺ had was well known for his honesty. People used to call him "Al-Amin," meaning

## Life of the Prophet Muhammad ﷺ

"the honest one." He was known among the people of Makkah as the bravest and most gentlemanly person. He was a good neighbor, tolerant and always truthful. He always kept aloof from quarrels and quibbles, and never used foul or abusive language.

The Prophet Muhammad ﷺ was employed by a wealthy widow, Khadijah. Muhammad ﷺ handled her business very well and visited Syria to trade her goods. Later the Prophet Muhammad married Khadijah. They were blessed with six children, two boys and four girls. Sadly, both sons died at an early age. Khadijah was not only the Prophet Muhammad's wife, but also his friend and helper and later, his first disciple.

Soon the Prophet Muhammad ﷺ gave up all worldly activities and set himself to searching for the truth. Often he would stay alone for days in the cave of Hira, near Makkah, to pray and meditate. He would wonder: "What does the Lord require from us? From where does man come, and where will he go after death? What is man's true role in life?"

One night during Ramadan, when Muhammad ﷺ was sitting all alone in the cave, an angel appeared and taught him the first verses of the Quran beginning with the line, "Read: In the name of Your Lord who created..." In this way the Quran began to be revealed by Allah to the Prophet Muhammad through the angel, whose name was Jibril (Gabriel). It took 23 years to complete the revelations of the Quran.

In this way Allah chose the Prophet Muhammad ﷺ as His Last Prophet and Messenger for all of humanity. The Archangel Jibril would come to the Prophet in different forms, sometimes like a man, sometimes like a huge bird, filling the whole sky, spreading his wings from east to west.

## Life of the Prophet Muhammad

As soon as the Prophet received the revelations of the Quran, he would instruct his companions to write them down. The Prophet would always keep one or more scribes with him to write down the divine messages as soon as they were revealed. At the same time the verses were memorized by many companions. In this way the Quran was written down right from day one, and compiled from beginning to end during the Prophet's lifetime.

When the Prophet Muhammad gave the message of Islam to the people of Makkah, most of them opposed him. Ultimately, the Makkan resistance to the Prophet's message brought hardship and torture to the Muslims. Some of the companions had to migrate to Abyssinia (Ethiopia). The Makkans even imposed a social ban on the Prophet's family. No one was to talk to them or do business with them. This ban lasted for three years, and caused the family great suffering.

One night as the Prophet slept next to the Kabah, the Archangel Jibril woke him up and took him on a strange, white winged animal, called Buraq (lightning), first from Makkah to al-Aqsa mosque in Jerusalem and then through the seven Heavens into the Divine Presence. The Prophet looked upon that which the eyes cannot see and minds cannot imagine, the Creator of heaven and earth. This experience, which took place in less than a moment, is called the Night Journey and the Ascension (al-Isra and al-Miraj).

Ultimately, to stamp out Islam, the Makkans hatched an evil plot to kill the Prophet. At the divine command, the Prophet left for Madinah along with Abu Bakr. The Makkans sent search parties to capture the Prophet. The Prophet and Abu Bakr took shelter in the cave of Thawr, outside Makkah. The enemy came very close to the mouth of the cave. But they left after seeing that a spider had spun a web across its opening and a dove had made a nest just to one side of it.

## Life of the Prophet Muhammad

The Prophet safely reached Madinah, and his journey is known as the Hijrah, or migration. Here he was warmly welcomed by the Ansars, or the Helpers, the people of Madinah. Slowly, almost all of the followers of the Prophet joined him in Madinah. The Prophet's migration to Madinah left the Makkans, feeling cheated of their prey, therefore, they fought with the Prophet at places such as Badr, Uhud, etc. Ultimately, the Prophet entered into a peace agreement with the Makkans at Hudaybiyyah, after which peace prevailed in the region.

The Prophet's Mosque in Madinah became the centre of his activities; he would sit there for hours and hours to give people the message of Islam. The Prophet's message spread far and wide. He sent letters with the basic message of Islam to neighboring kings. Slowly, tribe after tribe began to come into the fold of Islam. The numbers of tribesmen ran into thousands.

The Prophet Muhammad taught us that prayer is a way of saying how we need Allah's grace for every single thing we have, and how Allah's power over all things is total. He urged his followers to remember the Day of Judgement, when Allah will judge our actions by punishing the wicked and rewarding those who followed His path. He also urged his followers to spend time in prayer and in remembrance of Allah, and to live kindly and humbly, releasing slaves, giving in charity, especially to very poor people, to orphans and the needy, without any thought of reward.

The Prophet Muhammad's life went through various stages of well-being and extreme hardship, yet never once did he stray from the path of moderation. At all times, and right till the end, he remained the patient and grateful servant of the Almighty, bringing his message of peace and tolerance to all mankind.

# Doing *wudu* or ablutions for prayer

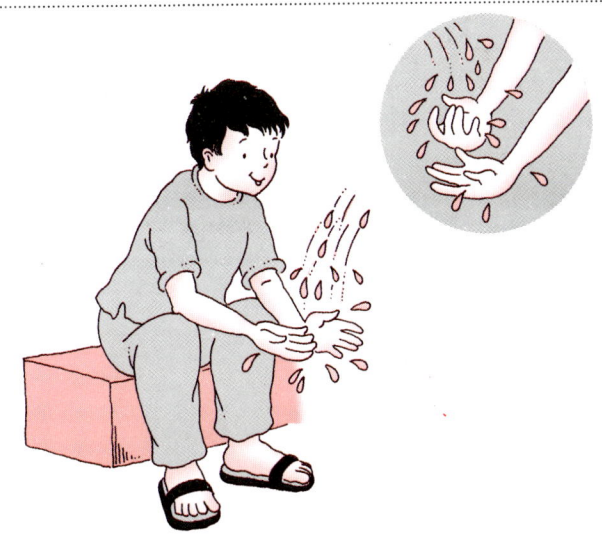

1. Say: "Bismillah!" Wash both hands completely up to the wrist.

2. Rinse the mouth thoroughly, sniff water into the nose and blow it out.

**Doing *wudu* or ablutions for prayer**

3. Wash the face completely.

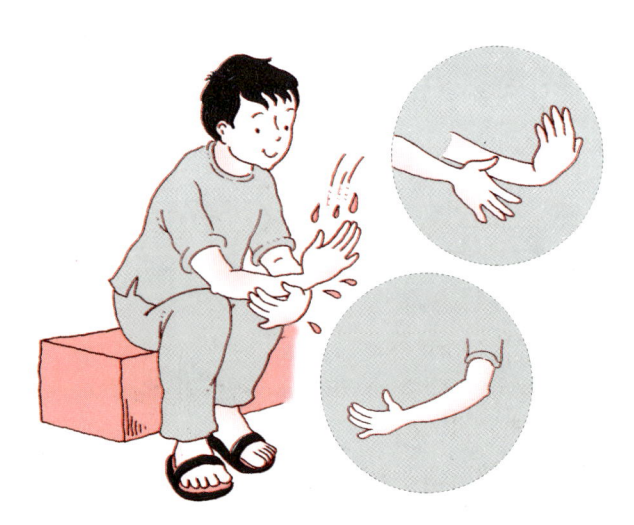

4. First wash your right hand and forearm, including the elbow.

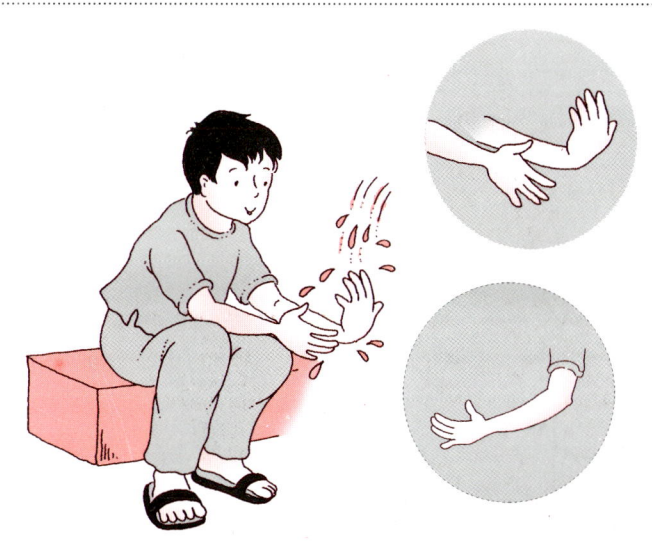

**Doing *wudu* or ablutions for prayer**

5. Then wash your left hand and forearm, including the elbow.

6. Pass both your wet hands over your head, from front to back and from back to front.

**Doing *wudu* or ablutions for prayer**

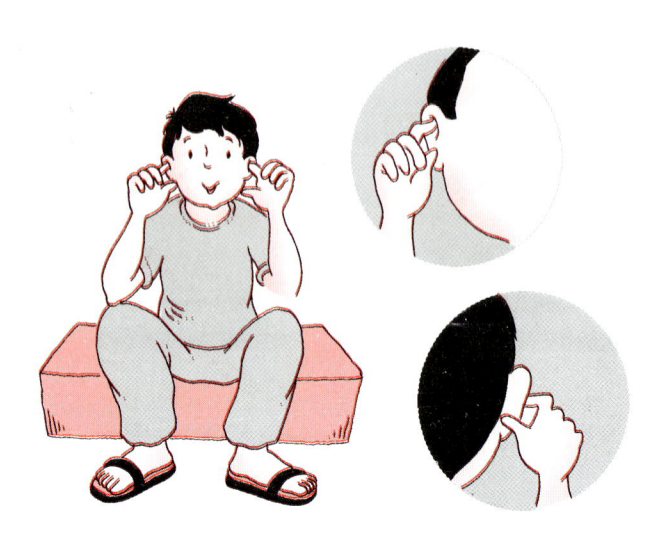

7. Wipe your ears with your fingers inside and out.

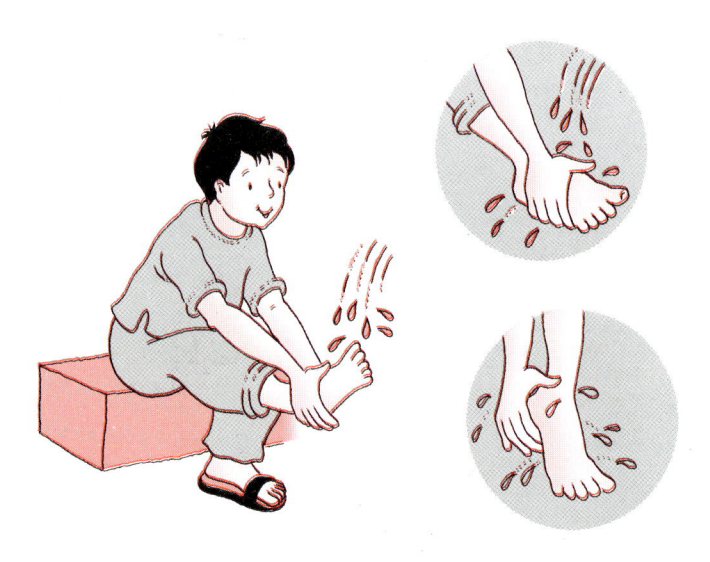

8. First wash your right foot thoroughly, including the ankle.

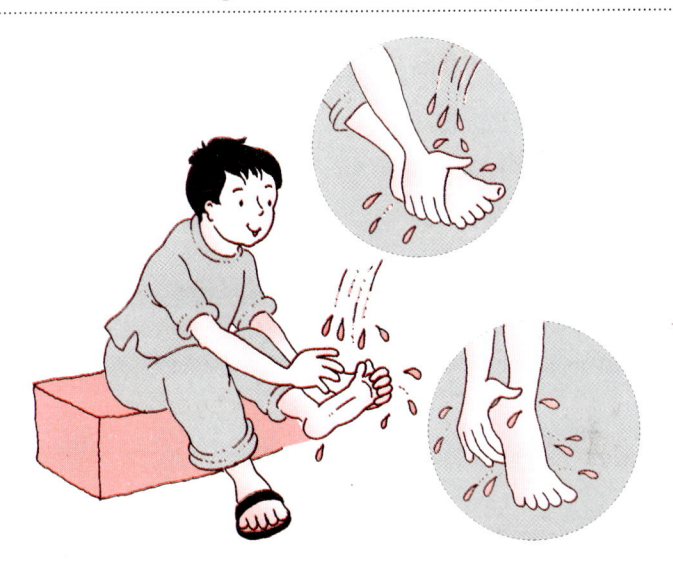

**Doing *wudu* or ablutions for prayer**

9. Then wash your left foot thoroughly, including the ankle.

Now say:
Ana ashhadu an la ilaha illal-lah
wa ashhadu anna Muhammadar rasulul-lah.

(This unit is based on the book, *My Wudu Book*, published by Darussalam Publishers & Distributors, Riyadh)

# How to say your prayers

Before offering prayers or *salat*, perform ablutions (*wudu*) to make sure that you have a clean body, make sure that you are in a clean place and that you are wearing clean clothes. Now stand upright on your prayer mat and face in the direction of the Kabah, which is called *qiblah*.

The following is the way to offer prayers:

1. Make known your intention (*niyyah*): "I intend to pray 2 (3 or 4) *rakahs fard* (or *sunnah*, etc.) of the dawn (*fajr*), noon (*zuhr*), afternoon (*'asr*), sunset (*maghrib*) or night (*'isha*) prayer for Allah, facing toward the Kabah."

## How to say your prayers

2. Say أَللهُ أَكْبَرُ "Allahu Akbar," raising your hands to your ears (up to the shoulders for ladies) and place the right hand on the left hand just below the navel or on the lower chest (on the chest for ladies).

3. Now recite:

سُبْحٰنَكَ اللّٰهُمَّ وَبِحَمْدِكَ وَتَبَارَكَ اسْمُكَ وَتَعَالٰى جَدُّكَ وَلَآ اِلٰهَ غَيْرُكَ ۰
اَعُوْذُ بِاللّٰهِ مِنَ الشَّيْطٰنِ الرَّجِيْمِ ۰ بِسْمِ اللّٰهِ الرَّحْمٰنِ الرَّحِيْمِ ۰

*Subhanaka Allahumma wa bi hamdika wa tabaraka'smuka wa ta'ala jadduka wa la ilaha ghairuk. A'udhu billahi minash-shaitanir-rajim. Bismillahir-rahmanir-rahim.*

**How to say your prayers**

Allah, all glory and praise belong to You alone. Blessed is Your name and exalted is Your Majesty, there is no god but You!

I seek refuge in Allah from the cursed Satan. In the name of Allah, the Compassionate, the Merciful.

4. After this, recite the first chapter of the Qur'an, the *surah al-Fatiha*;

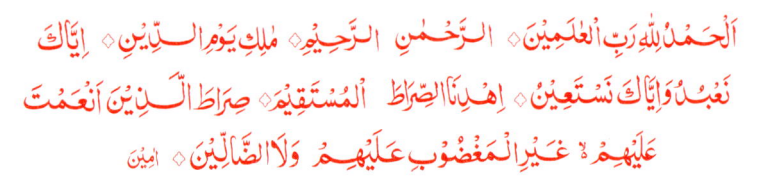

اَلْحَمْدُ لِلّٰهِ رَبِّ الْعٰلَمِيْنَ ۙ الرَّحْمٰنِ الرَّحِيْمِ ۙ مٰلِكِ يَوْمِ الدِّيْنِ ۙ اِيَّاكَ نَعْبُدُ وَاِيَّاكَ نَسْتَعِيْنُ ۙ اِهْدِنَا الصِّرَاطَ الْمُسْتَقِيْمَ ۙ صِرَاطَ الَّذِيْنَ اَنْعَمْتَ عَلَيْهِمْ ۙ غَيْرِ الْمَغْضُوْبِ عَلَيْهِمْ وَلَا الضَّآلِّيْنَ ۙ اٰمِيْن

*Alhamdu lillahi rabbil-alamin, ar rahmanir-rahim. Maliki yawmiddin. Iyyaka na'budu wa iyyaka nastain. Ihdinassiratal-mustaqim. Siratal-ladhina anamta alayhim, ghayril-maghdhubi alayhim waladhdhalin. Amin.*

Praise be to Allah, Lord of the Universe. The Compassionate, the Merciful. Master of the Day of Judgment. You alone we worship, and to You alone we turn for help. Guide us to the straight path. The path of those whom You have favoured. Not of those who have incurred Your wrath nor of those who have gone astray.

5. Add one of the short *surahs* of the Qur'an such as *surah 112, al-Ikhlas*:

**How to say your prayers**

قُلْ هُوَاللّٰهُ اَحَدٌ ۞ اَللّٰهُ الصَّمَدُ ۞ لَمْ يَلِدْ ۞ وَلَمْ يُولَدْ ۞ وَلَمْ يَكُنْ لَهُ كُفُوًا اَحَدٌ ۞

*Qul huallahu ahad. Allahussamad,
lam yalid walam yulad,
walam yakullahu kufuwan ahad.*

Say: He is Allah, the One and Only, Allah, the Eternal, Absolute; He begot none, nor was He begotten. And there is none equal to Him.

6. Now say, اللّٰهُ اَكْبَرُ "Allahu Akbar," bowing down and placing both hands on the knees, (the posture known as *ruku*) then say three or five times, سُبْحٰنَ رَبِّيَ الْعَظِيْمِ "Subhana rabbiyal-adhim." (Glory be to my Lord, the Most High).

**How to say your prayers**

7. Rising now to the standing position, say: سَمِعَ اللهُ لِمَنْ حَمِدَهُ "Sami' Allahu liman hamidah." (Allah listens to him who praises Him). In congregational prayers, when the imam says this phrase, the congregation says in response: رَبَّنَا لَكَ الْحَمْدُ "Rabbana lakal hamd." (Our Lord, to You belongs praise!).

8. Saying اللهُ أَكْبَرُ "Allahu Akbar," prostrate yourself on the floor, touching your forehead to the ground and with both palms on the ground. In this position, which is called *sajda*, say silently

three or five times: سُبْحَنَ رَبِّيَ الْأَعْلَى "Subhana rabbiyal-a'la" (Glory to my Lord, the Most High).

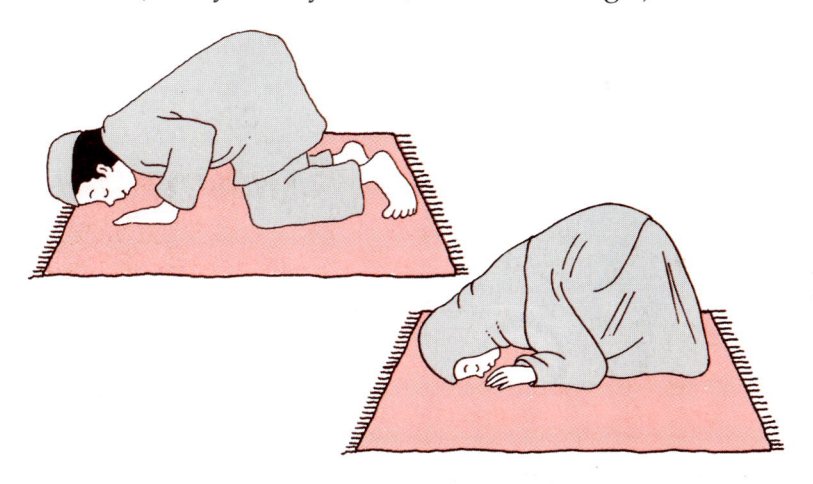

Now rise to the seated position saying, اَللَّهُ أَكْبَرُ "Allahu Akbar," and then make the second prostration, saying, اَللَّهُ أَكْبَرُ "Allahu Akbar" and repeat: سُبْحَنَ رَبِّيَ الْأَعْلَى "Subhana rabbiyal-ala." Get up from this position saying, اَللَّهُ أَكْبَرُ "Allahu Akbar." This completes one *rakah*. The second *rakah* will be performed in the same way, except that steps 1, 2 and 3 will not be repeated.

9. After completion of the second *rakah*, sit upright and recite:

اَلتَّحِيَّاتُ لِلّٰهِ وَالصَّلَوَاتُ وَالطَّيِّبَاتُ اَلسَّلَامُ عَلَيْكَ أَيُّهَا النَّبِيُّ وَرَحْمَةُ اللّٰهِ وَبَرَكَاتُهُ ، اَلسَّلَامُ عَلَيْنَا وَعَلَىٰ عِبَادِ اللّٰهِ الصَّالِحِينَ ، أَشْهَدُ أَنْ لَّا إِلٰهَ إِلَّا اللّٰهُ وَأَشْهَدُ أَنَّ مُحَمَّدًا عَبْدُهُ وَرَسُولُهُ ،

*At-tahiyyatu lillahi was-salawatu wat-tayyibatu. Assalamu alaika ayyuhannabiyyu wa rahmatullahi wa barkatuhu. Assalamu alaina wa ala ibadillahis-salihin.*

**How to say your prayers**

*Ashhadu an la ilaha illal Lahu wa ashhadu anna Muhammadan abduhu wa rasuluhu.*

Salutation, prayers and good works are all for Allah. Let there be peace, Allah's mercy and blessings on you, O Prophet. Peace be on us and on all Allah's righteous servants. I testify that there is no god but Allah, and I testify that Muhammad is His servant and His Messenger.

If the *salat* has more than two *rakahs*, then stand up for the remaining *rakah(s)* and perform the same way except the steps 1, 2, 3 and 5. Or, if it is a two-*rakah* prayer, remain seated and recite, the supplication called *qunut*:

اَللّٰهُمَّ صَلِّ عَلَىٰ مُحَمَّدٍ وَعَلَىٰ اٰلِ مُحَمَّدٍ كَمَا صَلَّيْتَ عَلَىٰ اِبْرَاهِيْمَ وَعَلَىٰ اٰلِ اِبْرَاهِيْمَ اِنَّكَ حَمِيْدٌ مَّجِيْدٌ ۔

**How to say your prayers**

*Allahumma salli ala Muhammadin wa ala ali Muhammadin kama sallayta ala Ibrahima wa ala ali Ibrahima innaka hamidum majid.*

Allah, bless Muhammad and the family of Muhammad, as You blessed Ibrahim (Abraham) and his family, for You are the Praiseworthy and the Glorious.

اَللّٰهُمَّ بَارِكْ عَلٰى مُحَمَّدٍ وَعَلٰى اٰلِ مُحَمَّدٍ كَمَا بَارَكْتَ عَلٰى اِبْرَاهِيْمَ وَعَلٰى اٰلِ اِبْرَاهِيْمَ اِنَّكَ حَمِيْدٌ مَّجِيْدٌ ۔

*Allahumma barik ala Muhammadin wa ala ali Muhammadin kama barakta ala Ibrahima wa ala ali Ibrahima innaka hamidum majid.*

Allah, bless Muhammad and the family of Muhammad, as You blessed Ibrahim and the family of Ibrahim; for You are the Praised, the Magnified.

اَللّٰهُمَّ اِنِّىْ ظَلَمْتُ نَفْسِىْ ظُلْمًا كَثِيْرًا وَلَا يَغْفِرُ الذُّنُوْبَ اِلَّا أَنْتَ فَاغْفِرْلِىْ مَغْفِرَةً مِّنْ عِنْدِكَ وَارْحَمْنِىْ اِنَّكَ اَنْتَ الْغَفُوْرُ الرَّحِيْمُ ۔

*Allahumma inni zalamtu nafsi zulman kathiran wa la yaghfirudh dhunuba illa anta faghfirli maghfiratan min indika wa rhamni innaka antal ghafurur-rahim.*

Allah, I have been unjust to myself, too unjust. No one can grant pardon for my sins except You, so forgive me with Your forgiveness and have mercy on me, for You are the Forgiver, the Merciful.)

## How to say your prayers

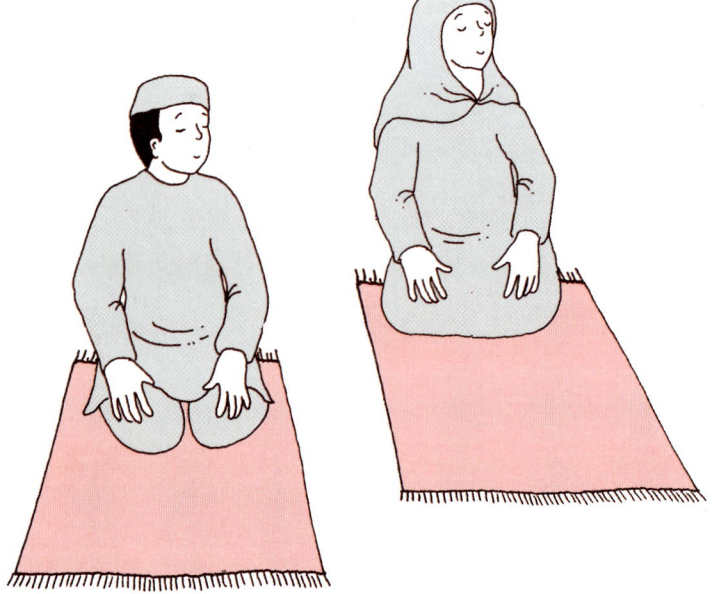

**How to say your prayers**

And now turn your face first to the right, then to the left, saying:

ٱلسَّلَامُ عَلَيْكُمْ وَرَحْمَةُ اللهِ

*Assalamu 'alaikum wa rahmatullah.*

Peace and the mercy of Allah be upon you.

This completes the *Salah*. Now it is the time for personal prayers. You may raise your hands and pray to Allah in your own words. However, here are some prayers for this purpose:

رَبَّنَا آتِنَا فِي الدُّنْيَا حَسَنَةً وَفِي الْآخِرَةِ حَسَنَةً وَقِنَا عَذَابَ النَّارِ

*Rabbana atina fiddunia hasanah wa fil-akhirati hasanah wa qina adhabannar.*

O our Lord, grant us good in this world and good in the Hereafter and save us from the punishment of the Hell-fire.

اَللّٰهُمَّ أَنْتَ السَّلَامُ وَمِنْكَ السَّلَامُ تَبَارَكْتَ يَا ذَا الْجَلَالِ وَالْإِكْرَامِ ۞

*Allahumma antas salamu wa minkas salamu tabarakata ya dhaljalali wal-ikram.*

O Allah, You are the source of peace and from You comes peace, exalted You are, O Lord of Majesty and Honour.

اَللّٰهُمَّ اغْفِرْلِيْ وَلِوَالِدَيَّ وَلِجَمِيْعِ الْمُؤْمِنِيْنَ وَالْمُؤْمِنَاتِ وَالْمُسْلِمِيْنَ وَالْمُسْلِمَاتِ بِرَحْمَتِكَ يَا أَرْحَمَ الرَّاحِمِيْنَ ۞

*Allahummaghfirli waliwalidaiyya wali jami'il mu'minina walmu'minati wal-muslimina wal-muslimati birahmatika ya arhamurrahimin.*

O Allah, forgive me and my parents and all the believing men and women and all Muslim men and women with Your mercy. O Most Merciful of all who have mercy.

رَبَّنَا ظَلَمْنَا أَنْفُسَنَا وَإِنْ لَمْ تَغْفِرْ لَنَا وَتَرْحَمْنَا لَنَكُوْنَنَّ مِنَ الْخَاسِرِيْنَ ۞

*Rabbana zalamna anfusana wa illam taghfirlana wa tarhamna lanakunanna minal-khasirin.*

Our Lord, we have wronged ourselves and if You do not forgive us and have no mercy on us, surely we will be of the losers.

# Names of surahs in the Qur'an

| Surah Number | Name of Surah in Arabic | English Meaning/Equivalent |
|---|---|---|
| 1 | al-Fatihah | The Opening |
| 2 | al-Baqarah | The Heifer |
| 3 | Al 'Imran | The Family of Imran |
| 4 | an-Nisa' | The Women |
| 5 | al-Ma'idah | The Table Spread |
| 6 | al-An'am | The Cattle |
| 7 | al-A'raf | The Heights |
| 8 | al-Anfal | The Spoils of War |
| 9 | al-Tawbah | The Repentance |
| 10 | Yunus | Jonah |
| 11 | Hud | — |
| 12 | Yusuf | Joseph |
| 13 | ar-Ra'd | The Thunder |
| 14 | Ibrahim | Abraham |
| 15 | al-Hijr | The Rocky Tract |
| 16 | an-Nahl | The Bee |
| 17 | al-Isra' | The Night Journey |
| 18 | al-Kahf | The Cave |
| 19 | Maryam | Mary |
| 20 | Ta Ha | — |
| 21 | al-Anbiya' | The Prophets |
| 22 | al-Hajj | The Pilgrimage |
| 23 | al-Mu'minun | The Believers |
| 24 | an-Nur | The Light |
| 25 | al-Furqan | The Criterion |

## Names of Surahs in the Qur'an

| | | |
|---|---|---|
| 26 | ash-Shu'ara' | The Poets |
| 27 | an-Naml | The Ants |
| 28 | al-Qasas | The Narrations |
| 29 | al-'Ankabut | The Spider |
| 30 | ar-Rum | The Romans |
| 31 | Luqman | — |
| 32 | as-Sajdah | The Prostration |
| 33 | al-Ahzab | The Confederates |
| 34 | Saba' | Sheba |
| 35 | Fatir | Originator |
| 36 | Ya Sin | — |
| 37 | as-Saffat | Those Ranged in Ranks |
| 38 | Sad | — |
| 39 | az-Zumar | The Crowds |
| 40 | Al-Mu'min | The Believer |
| 41 | Fussilat | Revelations Well Expounded |
| 42 | ash-Shura | The Consultation |
| 43 | az-Zukhruf | The Gold Adornments |
| 44 | ad-Dukhan | Smoke |
| 45 | al-Jathiyah | The Kneeling Down |
| 46 | al-Ahqaf | The Winding Sand-tracts |
| 47 | Muhammad | Muhammad |
| 48 | al-Fath | The Victory |
| 49 | al-Hujurat | The Inner Apartments |
| 50 | Qaf | — |
| 51 | adh-Dhariyat | The Winds That Scatter |
| 52 | at-Tur | The Mount |
| 53 | an-Najm | The Star |
| 54 | al-Qamar | The Moon |
| 55 | ar-Rahman | The Most Gracious |

## Names of Surahs in the Qur'an

| 56 | al-Waqi'ah | The Inevitable |
| 57 | al-Hadid | Iron |
| 58 | al-Mujadalah | The Pleading |
| 59 | al-Hashr | The Mustering, or Banishment |
| 60 | al-Mumtahnah | The Examined One |
| 61 | al-Saff | The Ranks |
| 62 | al-Jumu'ah | Friday, or the Day of Congregation |
| 63 | al-Munafiqun | The Hypocrites |
| 64 | at-Taghabun | Mutual Loss and Gain |
| 65 | at-Talaq | Divorce |
| 66 | at-Tahrim | Prohibition |
| 67 | al-Mulk | Dominion |
| 68 | al-Qalam | The Pen |
| 69 | al-Haqqah | The Catastrophe |
| 70 | al-Ma'arij | The Ways of Ascent |
| 71 | Nuh | Noah |
| 72 | al-Jinn | The Spirits |
| 73 | al-Muzzammil | The Enfolded One |
| 74 | al-Muddaththir | The Cloaked One |
| 75 | al-Qayamah | The Resurrection |
| 76 | al-Insan | Man |
| 77 | al-Mursalat | Those Sent Forth |
| 78 | an-Naba' | The Great News |
| 79 | an-Nazi'at | The Soul Snatchers |
| 80 | 'Abasa | He Frowned |
| 81 | at-Takwir | The Folding Up |
| 82 | al-Infitar | The Cleaving as under |
| 83 | al-Mutaffifin | The Unjust |
| 84 | al-Inshiqaq | The Rending Asunder |

## Names of Surahs in the Qur'an

| 85 | al-Buruj | The Constellations |
| 86 | at-Tariq | The Night-Visitant |
| 87 | al-A'la | The Most High |
| 88 | al-Ghashiyah | The Overwhelming Event |
| 89 | al-Fajr | The Break of Day |
| 90 | al-Balad | The City |
| 91 | ash-Shams | The Sun |
| 92 | al-Layl | Night |
| 93 | ad-Duha | The Glorious Morning Light |
| 94 | ash-Sharh | Comfort |
| 95 | at-Tin | The Fig |
| 96 | al-'Alaq | The Clinging Clot |
| 97 | al-Qadr | The Night of Glory |
| 98 | al-Bayyinah | Clear Evidence |
| 99 | az-Zalzalah | The Earthquake |
| 100 | al-'Adiyat | The Chargers |
| 101 | al-Qari'ah | The Great Calamity |
| 102 | at-Takathur | Worldly Gain |
| 103 | al-'Asr | The Declining Day |
| 104 | al-Humazah | The Scandalmonger |
| 105 | al-Fil | The Elephant |
| 106 | Quraysh | The Quraysh |
| 107 | al-Ma'un | Neighbourly Assistance |
| 108 | al-Kawthar | Abundance |
| 109 | al-Kafirun | Those Who Reject Faith |
| 110 | an-Nasr | Help |
| 111 | al-Masad | The Plaited Rope |
| 112 | al-Ikhlas | Purity of Faith |
| 113 | al-Falaq | Daybreak |
| 114 | an-Nas | Mankind |

# 99 Beautiful Names of Allah

1 Ar-Rahman (The Compassionate)
2 Ar-Rahim (The Merciful)
3 Al-Malik (The Sovereign)
4 Al-Quddus (The Holy)
5 As-Salam (The All-Peace)
6 Al-Mu'min (The Giver of Peace)
7 Al-Muhaymin (The Protector)
8 Al-'Aziz (The Almighty)
9 Al-Jabbar (The Irresistible)
10 Al-Mutakabbir (The Superb)
11 Al-Khaliq (The Creator)
12 Al-Bari (The Maker)
13 Al-Musawwir (The Shaper)
14 Al-Ghaffar (The Forgiving)
15 Al-Qahhar (The Dominant)
16 Al-Wahhab (The All-giving)
17 Ar-Razzaq (The All-provider)
18 Al-Fattah (The Opener)
19 Al-'Alim (The All-knowing)
20 Al-Qabiz (The Seizer)
21 Al-Basit (The Expander)
22 Al-Khafiz (The Abaser)
23 Ar-Rafi' (The Exalter)
24 Al-Mu'izz (The Honourer)

## 99 Beautiful Names of Allah

25  Al-Mudhill (The Humiliator)
26  As-Sami' (The All-hearing)
27  Al-Basir (The All-seeing)
28  Al-Hakam (The Judge)
29  Al-'Adl (The Just)
30  Al-Latif (The Subtle)
31  Al-Khabir (The All-aware)
32  Al-Halim (The All-clement)
33  Al- 'Azim (The All-glorius)
34  Al-Ghafur (The Forgiving)
35  Ash-Shakur (The Appreciative)
36  Al-'Ali (The Sublime)
37  Al-Kabir (The Great)
38  Al-Hafiz (The Guardian)
39  Al-Muqit (The Sustainer)
40  Al-Hasib (The Reckoner)
41  Al-Jalil (The Majestic)
42  Al-Karim (The Generous)
43  Ar-Raqib (The Watchful)
44  Al-Mujib (One who answers all)
45  Al-Wasi' (The All-embracing)
46  Al-Hakim (The Wise)
47  Al-Wadud (The Loving)
48  Al-Majid (The Glorious)
49  Al-Bais (The Resurrector)
50  Ash-Shahid (The Witness)

## 99 Beautiful Names of Allah

51  Al-Haqq (The Truth)
52  Al-Wakil (The Trustee)
53  Al-Qawi (The All-strong)
54  Al-Matin (The Firm)
55  Al-Wali (The Protector)
56  Al-Hamid (The Praiseworthy)
57  Al-Muhsi (The Reckoner)
58  Al-Mubdi (The Originator)
59  Al-Mu'id (The Restorer)
60  Al-Muhiyy (The Giver of life)
61  Al-Mumit (The Life-taker)
62  Al-Hayy (The Living)
63  Al-Qayyum (The Eternal)
64  Al-Wajid (The Finder)
65  Al-Majid (The Noble)
66  Al-Wahid (The One)
67  As-Samad (The Everlasting Refuge)
68  Al-Qadir (The Powerful)
69  Al-Muqtadir (The Prevailing)
70  Al-Muqaddim (The Promoter)
71  Al-Mua'khkhir (The Detainer)
72  Al-Awwal (The First)
73  Al-Akhir (The Last)
74  Az-Zahir (The Evident)
75  Al-Batin (The Hidden)
76  Al-Wali (The Protector)

## 99 Beautiful Names of Allah

77  Al-Muta 'ali (The All-exalted)
78  Al-Barr (The Beneficient)
79  At-Tawwab (The Acceptor of Repentance)
80  Al-Muntaqim (The Avenger)
81  Al-'Afuw (The Forgiving)
82  Ar-Ra'uf (The Gentle)
83  Malik ul-Mulk (The Lord of the Kingdom)
84  Zul Jalal-i-wa'l-Ikram (The Lord of Majesty and Generosity)
85  Al-Muqsit (The Just)
86  Al-Jami' (The Gatherer)
87  Al-Ghani (The Self-sufficient)
88  Al-Mughni (The Enricher)
89  Al-Mu'ti (The Giver)
90  Al-Mani' (The Withholder)
91  Al-Darr (The Afflicter)
92  An-Nafi' (The Beneficient)
93  An-Nur (The Light)
94  Al-Hadi (The Guide)
95  Al-Badi' (The Innovative Creator)
96  Al-Baqi (The Everlasting)
97  Al-Waris (The Inheritor)
98  Ar-Rashid (The Guide)
99  As-Sabur (The Forbearing)

# Names of the Prophet Muhammad ﷺ

| | |
|---|---|
| *'Abd Allāh* | The Servant of God |
| *Abū-l-Qāsim* | Father of Qasim |
| *Abū Ibrāhīm* | Father of Ibrahim |
| *Aḥmad* | The Most-Praised |
| *Ajmal Khalq Allāh* | The Most Beautiful of God's Creation |
| *'Alam al-Hudā* | The Banner of Guidance |
| *al-Amīn* | The Trustworthy |
| *'Ayn an-Na'īm* | The Fount of Blessings |
| *Bāligh* | The Proclaimer |
| *al-Bashīr* | The Bringer of Good Tidings |
| *al-Burhān* | The Proof |
| *Dalīl al-Khayrāt* | The Guide to Good Deeds |
| *Dār al-Ḥikmah* | The Abode of Wisdom |
| *Dhikr Allāh* | The Remembrance of God |
| *al-Fātiḥ* | The Opener |
| *al-Ghawth* | The Redeemer |
| *Ḥabīb Allāh* | The Beloved of God |
| *al-Ḥāshir* | The Gatherer (on the Day of Judgement) |
| *al-'Ilm al-Yaqīn* | The Knowledge that is Certitude |
| *Imām al-Muttaqīn* | The Model Leader of the |

## Names of the Prophet Muhammad ﷺ

|  |  |
|---|---|
|  | God-Fearing |
| *al-Kāmil* | The Perfect |
| *Kashif al-Karb* | The Effacer of Grief |
| *Khalīl ar-Raḥmān* | The Friend of the All-Compassionate |
| *Khātam an-Nabiyin* | The Seal of the Prophets |
| *Khātim ar-Rusul* | The Seal of the Messengers |
| *Madinat al-'Ilm* | The City of Knowledge |
| *al-Mahdī* | The Rightly-Guided |
| *al-Ma'sūm* | The Infalliable |
| *Miftāḥ al-Jannah* | The Key of Paradise |
| *Miftāḥ ar-Raḥmah* | The Key of Mercy |
| *al-Miṣbāḥ* | The Niche of Lights |
| *Muḥammad* | The Praised |
| *al-Muḥyī* | The Reviver |
| *al-Munīr* | The Illuminator |
| *al-Muṣṭāfā* | The Chosen |
| *an-Nabī* | The Prophet |
| *an-Nadhīr* | The Warner |
| *an-Najm ath-Thāqib* | The Piercing Star |
| *an-Nūr* | The Light |
| *al-Qamar* | The Moon |
| *Rāfi' ar-Ruṭab* | The Exalter of Ranks |
| *Raḥmah li-l-'Ālamīn* | The Mercy to the Universe |
| *Raḥmaṭ Allāh* | The Mercifulness of God |

## Names of the Prophet Muhammad

| | |
|---|---|
| *ar-Rasūl* | The Messenger |
| *Rūḥ al-Ḥaqq* | The Spirit of Truth |
| *Rūḥ al-Quddūs* | The Holy Spirit |
| *aṣ-Ṣādiq* | The Truthful |
| *Ṣāḥib al-Bayyān* | Master of the Clarification |
| *Ṣāḥib ad-Darajah ar-Rafīʻ* | The Truthful |
| *Ṣāḥib al-Miʻrāj* | He of the Night Ascent |
| *as-Sayyid* | The Liege Lord |
| *Sayyid al-Kawnayn* | Liege Lord of the Two Worlds |
| *Sayyid al-Mursalīn* | Liege Lord of the Messengers |
| *Shāfiʻ al-Mudhnibīn* | The Intercessor for Sinners |
| *ash-Shāhid* | The Witness |
| *ash-Shams* | The Sun |
| *ash-Shāriʻ* | The Legislator |
| *aṣ-Ṣirāṭ al-Mustaqīm* | The Straight Path |
| *Ṭāʼ Hāʼ* | (Sūrah of the Quran) |
| *aṭ-Ṭāhir* | The Pure |
| *aṭ-Ṭayyib* | The Good |
| *Wāli Allāh* | The Friend of God (The Saint) |
| *al-Wakīl* | The Advocate |
| *aṭ-Wāṣil* | The Joiner |
| *Yā ʻSīn* | (Sūrah of the Quran) |

# English names/words and their Arabic equivalents/meaning

| | | | |
|---|---|---|---|
| Aaron | Harun | Genii | Jinn |
| Abel | Habil | Gog | Yajuj |
| Abraham | Ibrahim | Goliath | Jalut |
| Adam | Adam | Gospel | Injil |
| Angel | Malak | Grave | Qabr |
| Apostle | Rasul | Hagar | Hajar |
| Benjamin | Binyamin | Hell | Jahannam |
| Cain | Qabil | Hypocrites | Munafiq |
| Caliph | Khalifah | Imran | 'Imran |
| Daniel | Daniyal | Isaac | Ishaq |
| David | Dawud | Ishmael | Isma'il |
| Eden | 'Adn | Israel | Isra'il |
| Elijah | Isyas | Jacob | Ya'qub |
| Elisha | Al-Yasa' | Jesus | 'Isa |
| Enoch | Idris | Jesus Christ | 'Isa al-Masih |
| Eve | Hawwa' | Jew | Yahudi |
| Ezekiel | Dhu'l-Kifl | Job | Ayyub |
| Ezra | 'Uzayr | John | Yahya |
| Gabriel | Jibra'il or Jibril | Jonah | Yunus |

**English Names/Words and their Arabic Equivalents/Meaning**

| | | | |
|---|---|---|---|
| Joseph | Yusuf | Omiades | Umayyads |
| Joshua | Yusha' | Osman | 'Uthman |
| Koran | Qur'an | Paradise | Jannah |
| Lot | Lut | Pharaoh | Fir'awn |
| Magog | Majuj | Philosophy | Falsafah |
| Mecca | Makkah | Pilgrimage | Hajj |
| Medina | Madinah | Prayer | Salah |
| Michael | Mika'il | Prophet | Nabi |
| Midian | Madyan | Psalms | Zabur |
| Moses | Musa | Sheba | Saba |
| Mosque | Masjid | Sabeans | Sabi'un |
| Nimrod | Namrud | Satan | Shaytan |
| Noah | Nuh | Solomon | Sulayman |
| Ohud | Uhud | Tradition | Hadith |
| Omer | 'Umar | Zacharias | Zakariyyah |

# Adhan or Call to Prayer

Adhan is made by a muadhdhin from the minaret of a mosque, five times daily to call the Muslims for the ritual prayers. The words of adhan are:

Allahu Akbar (Allah is Great) – four times,

Ashhadu alla ilaha illah (I witness that there is no deity but Allah) – twice,

Ashhadu anna Muhammadar-Rasulullah (I witness that Muhammad is the Messenger of Allah) – twice,

Hayya 'ala-s-salah (Come to prayer) – twice,

Hayya 'ala-l-falah (Come to salvation) – twice,

Allahu Akbar (Allah is Great) – twice,

La ilaha illallah (There is no deity but Allah) – once.

For the early morning adhan, the following is added between hayya 'ala-l-falah and Allahu Akbar:

As-salatu khayrum-min an-nawm (Prayer is better than sleep) – twice.

# Chronology of Islam

| | |
|---|---|
| c. 570 c.e. | Birth of the Prophet Muhammad in Makkah. |
| 619 | Death of Khadijah, first wife of the Prophet and first convert to Islam. |
| 622 | The Hijrah: the emigration of the Prophet Muhammad and his followers from Makkah to Madinah, marking the beginning of the Islamic lunar calendar. |
| 630 | Conquest of Makkah. |
| 632 | The Farewell Pilgrimage and death of the Prophet. |
| 632 | Death of Fatimah, daughter of the Prophet and wife of Ali. |
| 632-4 | Caliphate of Abu Bakr. |
| 634-44 | Caliphate of 'Umar. |
| 635 | Conquest of Damascus. |
| 639 | Conquest of Egypt. |
| 640 | Conquest of Persia. |
| 644 | Death of 'Umar. |
| 644-56 | Caliphate of 'Uthman. |
| 651 | Death of the last pre-Islamic Persian emperor, Yazdigird. |
| 653 | Official date of the canonization of the Qur'an under 'Uthman. |

## Chronology of Islam

| | |
|---|---|
| 656 | Death of 'Uthman. |
| 656-61 | Caliphate of 'Ali. |
| 657 | Battle of Siffin between supporters of Ali and the army of Mu'awiyyah. |
| 661 | Assassination of 'Ali. Mu'awiyyah becomes Caliph. |
| 661-750 | Umayyad dynasty. |
| 678 | Death of A'ishah, wife of the Prophet and one of the most influential figures in early Islam. |
| 680 | Husayn, son of Ali and grandson of the Prophet, martyred at Karbalah. |
| 711 | Conquest of Spain. |
| 711-12 | Conquest of the Indus Valley. |
| 750 | Defeat of the Umayyads by the Abbasid dynasty. |
| 762 | The city of Baghdad founded as the seat of the Caliphate and capital of the Abbasids. |
| 765 | Death of Ja'far as-Sadiq, the sixth Shi'ite Imam. He is the last Imam to be recognized by both the "Twelver" Shi'ites and the Isma'ilis, and is highly regarded for his religious knowledge. |
| 767 | Death of the great legal scholar, Abu Hanifah. |
| 784-6 | Building of the Great Mosque in Cordoba, Spain. |
| 786-809 | Reign of the famous caliph, Harun al-Rashid. |

## Chronology of Islam

| | |
|---|---|
| 801 | Death of the ascetic mystic, Rabi'ah al-Adawiyah. |
| 813-33 | Reign of the Abbasid caliph al-Ma'mun, under whom there was a great flowering in Islamic scholarship and literature. Major theological debate over the nature of the Qur'an. |
| 817 | Attempt at reconciling Shi'ite and Sunni Islamic sects. |
| 820 | Death of al-Shafi'i, a famous legal scholar. |
| 855 | Death of the theologian and legal scholar, Ibn Hanbal. |
| 870 | Death of Bukhari, the famous compiler of Hadith. |
| 874 | The twelfth Imam of the "Twelver" Shi'ites, Muhammad al-Qa'im, disappears from the world. He is not expected to return until the events that signal the end of this world. |
| 875 | Death of Muslim Ibn al-Hajjaj, the famous compiler of Hadith. |
| 890 | First appearance of Isma'ili religious and political insurgents in Iraq. |
| c. 900 | Rise of Zaydi Shi'ism in Yemen. |
| 928 | Raid on Makkah and desecration of the Ka'bah by the extremist Isma'ili followers of Hamdan Qarmat. |
| 935 | Death of the great theologian, al-Ash'ari. |
| 950 | Death of the philosopher, al-Farabi. |
| 970 | Foundation of the Al-Azhar mosque in Cairo. |

## Chronology of Islam

| | |
|---|---|
| 1037 | Death of the philosopher, Ibn Sina (known as Avicenna in the West). |
| 1064 | Death of Ibn Hazm, a theologian, philosopher, poet, and jurisprudent, and possibly the greatest scholar to come out of Islamic Spain. |
| 1075 | Battle of Manzikert, in which the Seljuk Turks defeated the Byzantine army and captured the Byzantine Emperor Romanus Diogenus, thereby opening the Byzantine territories to future invasion and conquest. |
| 1099 | Crusaders capture Jerusalem. |
| 1111 | Death of the famous theologian, Al-Ghazali. |
| 1153 | Death of Muhammad al-Shahrastani, a historian of religion famous for his *Book of Religions and Sects*. |
| 1187 | Retaking of Jerusalem from the Crusaders by Salah al-Din. |
| 1198 | Death of the great Spanish philosopher, Ibn Rushd (known as Averroes in the West). |
| 1220 | The Mongol invasion of the Islamic world. |
| 1240 | Death of the great Spanish mystical philosopher, Ibn al-Arabi. |
| 1258 | Mongol conquest of Baghdad and the end of the Abbasid Caliphs. |
| 1260 | Battle of Ayn Jalut, at which the Egyptian Mamluks defeated the Mongols, preventing them from invading Africa. |

## Chronology of Islam

| | |
|---|---|
| 1273 | Death of the famous mystical poet, Jalal al-din Rumi. |
| 1453 | Conquest of Constantinople by the Ottoman Turks, who renamed it Istanbul. |
| late 1400s | Muslim communities established in southern West Africa. |
| 1492 | The fall of Granada and the end of the last Muslim principality in Spain. |
| 1501-24 | Reign of Shah Isma'il I, a founder of the Safavid Empire in Iran. |
| 1502 | "Twelver" Shi'ism is made the official religion of Iran. |
| 1505 | Death of Al-Suyuti, a famous Egyptian historian, grammarian, and scholar of the Qur'an. |
| 1517 | Ottoman conquest of Egypt, after which the Ottoman emperor also claims to be the Caliph of the Islamic world. |
| 1520-66 | Reign of Ottoman emperor Sulayman the Magnificent, who makes the Ottoman claim to be the main rulers of the Sunni Islamic world a reality. |
| 1526-30 | Reign of the Emperor Babur, who laid the foundations of the Mughal Empire in India. |
| c. 1550 | Islam arrives in Cambodia. |
| mid-1500s | Islam becomes established in Borneo. |
| 1550-7 | Construction of the Sulaymani mosque in Istanbul. |

## Chronology of Islam

| | |
|---|---|
| 1609-14 | The expulsion of all Muslims from Spain. |
| 1624 | Death of the Indian mystic and reformer Ahmad Sirhindi. |
| 1744 | Alliance between the religious reformer Ibn Abd al-Wahhab and Muhammad Ibn Sa'ud, which eventually led to the creation of Saudi Arabia. |
| 1792 | Death of Abd al-Wahhab. |
| 1798 | Napoleon invades Egypt. |
| 1817 | Death of Usuman Dan Fodio, founder of the Sokoto Caliphate. |
| 1897 | Death of the reformer Jamal ad-Din al-Afghani. |
| 1898 | Death of the reformer Sayyid Ahmad Khan. |
| 1906 | Constitutional reform in Iran. |
| 1917 | Abolition of the Sunni caliphate. |
| 1924 | Turkey becomes the first Muslim-majority secular republic. |
| 1939 | Death of the philosopher and poet Muhammad Iqbal. |
| 1966 | Death of the Islamist reformer Sayyid Qutb. |
| 1990 | Dissolution of the Soviet Union gives independence to Muslim-majority Soviet republics that had formerly been Russian colonies. |

# Notable Muslims

**Abu Bakr "al-Siddiq",** ca. 570-634: One of the first followers of the Prophet who, in 632, became the first of the four "rightly guided" caliphs.

**'Umar ibn al-Khattab,** 592-644: Second of the four "rightly guided" caliphs. He originated most of the major political institutions of the Muslim state and helped stabilize the rapidly expanding Arab empire.

**'Uthman ibn Affan,** d. 656: Third of the "rightly guided" caliphs, married successively to two of the Prophet's daughters. Elected caliph in 644, he ordered the official collation of the Qur'an.

**'Ali ibn Abi Talib,** ca. 596-661: Cousin and son-in-law of the Prophet Muhammad. In 656 he became the last of the "rightly guided" caliphs.

**Harun al-Rashid,** 786-809: Fifth caliph of the Abbasid empire, he ruled during its apogee, as described in *The 1001 Nights*. Founder, with his son and successor al-Ma'mun, 813-833, of the Bayt al-Hikmah, or House of Wisdom, in Baghdad, where Greek classics were translated, studied and preserved.

**Ziryab (Abu al-Hasan 'Ali ibn Nafi)** b. 789: Baghdadi musician, *'ud* (lute) master and cultural innovator who became chief musician and *arbiter* of fashion at the court of Abd al-Rahman II in Cordoba in 822.

**Muslim ibn al-Hajjaj,** 817-875: Collector of the traditions of the Prophet Muhammad (*hadith*).

## Notable Muslims

**Muhammad ibn Musa al-Khwarizmi,** ca. 800-847: Mathematician, astronomer, geographer of Baghdad. He introduced algebra and Indian/Arabic numerals—as well as the words *algebra* and *algorithm*—to Europe in the 12th century.

**Muhammad ibn Ismail al-Bukhari,** 810-870: Compiler of *Hadith*.

**Zubayda,** d. 831: Wife of Harun al-Rashid. Sponsored mosques, hostelries and schools and backed improvements to the pilgrims' road from Kufa to Makkah, called the *darb Zubayda.* (Zubayda's Road.)

**Abu Bakr Muhammad ibn Zakariya al-Razi,** 841-926: Physician, philosopher, alchemist, musician and mathematician, born in Rayy, Persia. Called Rhazes in the West. Islam's greatest physician and most freethinking philosopher, author of more than 200 books, including the first pediatric work, the first treatise on small pox and measles, and a 25-volume medical survey.

**Firdawsi (Abu'l-Qasim Mansur),** 940-1020: Great Persian poet, author of the 60,000-verse *Shahnama* (*Book of Kings*), the Persian national epic.

**Abu 'Ali al-Hasan ibn al-Hasan ibn al-Haytham,** 965-1040: Combined physical doctrines with mathematics. Known in the West as **Alhazen.** Wrote the *Kitab al-Manazir* (*On Optics*), in which he proposed a new theory of vision. Influenced Kepler and Descartes; extended Euclid's *Elements*.

**Abu al-Rayhan Muhammad ibn Ahmad al-Biruni,** 973-1048: Astronomer, mathematician, geographer, physicist, historian.

Born in (today's) Uzbekistan, he wrote *A History of India*, and *A Chronology of Ancient Nations* as well as other major works.

**Abu 'Ali al-Husayn ibn 'Abd Allah ibn Sina,** 980-1037: The "Leonardo da Vinci of the Muslim world," known as Avicenna in the West. Born in Bukhara, (today's) Uzbekistan. Wrote on theology, metaphysics, astronomy, philology, poetry, and medicine, including *Al-Qanun fi al-Tibb* (*The Canon of Medicine*), a codification of all existing medical knowledge that was used as a reference in Europe well into the 15th century.

**'Aishah bint Ahmad al-Qurtubiya,** ca. 1000: Famed woman poet and calligrapher of Andalusia.

**Omar Khayyam,** ca. 1048-1125: Persian mathematician, astronomer and poet best known for the *Rubaiyat;* also helped reform the solar calendar.

**Abu Hamid Muhammad al-Ghazali,** 1058-1111: Persian astronomer, jurist, philosopher and mystic; Algazel to the West. Author of some 70 works, al-Ghazali won early fame as a lawyer in Baghdad but later relinquished his post to pursue the nature of knowledge.

**Abu Marwan 'Abd al-Malik ibn Zuhr,** 1091-1162: Physician, born Seville. Known to the West as Avenzoar and renowned for his surgical skills.

**Wallada bint al-Mustakfi,** d. ca. 1091: Poet of Umayyad Cordoba famous for her wit and eloquence, literary parties and love poetry.

**Abu 'Abd Allah Muhammad al-Idrisi,** 1099-1180: Geographer, born Ceuta, Morocco and educated in Cordoba.

Served in the court of Roger II of Sicily, for whom he produced *al-Kitab al-Rujari,* a geographical treatise which included the first scientific map of the world.

**Abu al-Walid Muhammad ibn Rushd,** 1126-1198: Philosopher, physician, jurist. Known as Averroes in the West. Active in Seville, Cordoba and Marrakech. "The Great Commentator" on Aristotle whose works, translated into Latin, gave Europeans their first substantive introduction to Greek philosophy.

**Salah al-Din al-Ayyubi,** 1138-1193: Founder of Ayyubid dynasty of Egypt and Syria; known as Saladin in the West. Ejected the Crusaders from Jerusalem in 1187 and garnered fame through chivalric battles with Richard the Lion-Heart.

**Muhyi 'l-Din al-Ta'i ibn al-'Arabi,** 1165-1240: Mystic, born in Murcia, Spain. Author of some 400 works, including a summary of the teaching of 28 prophets from Adam to Muhammad.

**Hafsa bint al-Hajj al-Rakuni,** ca. 12th c. Greatest woman poet of al-Andalus.

**Badi' al-Zaman Isma'il ibn al-Razzaz al-Jazari,** ca. 1150-1200: Engineer, inventor. His prescient *Book of Knowledge of Ingenious Mechanical Devices* gives detailed descriptions and drawings of clocks, irrigation machines, fountains, automata, and other technologies.

**Jalal al-Din Rumi,** 1207-1273: Mystic, poet, born in Balkh, (today's) Afghanistan. After his death, his disciples organised the Mevlevi order, sometimes called the "whirling dervishes."

## Notable Muslims

**Ib al-Nafis,** d. 1288: Physician of Damascus. Wrote compendium of Arab knowledge of ophthalmology. Proposed the theory of the pulmonary circulation of the blood.

**'Abd al-Rahman ibn Khaldun,** 1332-1406: Historian, sociologist. Born in Tunis, he served at courts in Andalusia and North Africa and taught at al-Azhar in Cairo. Author of *Kitab al-'Ibar* (*Universal History*), in which he treated history as a science and outlined reasons for the rise and fall of civilizations.

**Timur (Tamerlane),** ca. 1336-1405: Conqueror of an empire that included all or parts of today's Afghanistan, Persia, India, Turkey, Syria and Egypt. Equally famed for ruthlessness and the monuments he commissioned, especially in his capital, Samarqand.

**Sinan,** 1488-1587: Master architect of the Ottoman empire who designed, among many others, the Sulaymaniya Mosque in Istanbul and the Selimiye Mosque in Edirne.

**Sulayman I,** 1494-1566: Ottoman Sultan who guided the empire to the fullest extent of its power and prestige. A patron of the arts and sponsor of vast public works; the present city walls of Jerusalem are one of his many projects in that city alone.

**Shihab al-Din ibn Majid,** 15th c.: Navigator on Vasco da Gama's voyage from Portugal to India in 1497-1498.

**Mirza Asadullah Ghalib,** 1797-1869: Great poet of India, father of modern Urdu prose.

## Notable Muslims

**Jamal al-Din al-Afghani,** 1838-1897: Journalist, reformer. A founder of modern Muslim anti-colonialism, he advocated a religious and cultural revival to counteract European influence.

**Muhammad Iqbal,** 1876-1938: Poet, philosopher, jurist and social reformer. He advocated the creation of a Muslim state in north-west India.

**Naguib Mahfouz,** b. 1911: Egyptian writer, winner of the Nobel Prize for literature in 1988. His work features realistic depictions of middle and lower class Egyptians.

**Malcolm X.** 1925-1965: American civil rights leader.

**Muhammad Ali,** b. 1942: Three-time world heavyweight champion boxer; became a Muslim in 1964.

**Ahmed H. Zewail,** b. 1946: Egyptian-born American chemist, winner of the 1999 Nobel Prize for imaging chemical interactions on an atomic scale.

*(Adapted from Saudi Aramco World)*

# Suggestions for Reading

Readers who want to learn more about Islam will find interesting material in this list. Some of the titles are recent, some are classic, and others did not get the attention they deserved when they were published. Most of the books listed here are available from Goodword Books Pvt. Ltd., 1, Nizamuddin West Market, New Delhi-110013, Tel. 24355454, 24356666, Fax: 91 11-2435 7333, 2435 7980, e-mail: info@goodwordbooks.com

**A-Z Guide to the Qur'an,** Mokhtar Stork, Times Books International, 981-204-739-5, pb.

**Allah is Known Through Reason**, Harun Yahya, Goodword Books, 81-87570-05-9, pb.

**Arabic-English Dictionary**, J.G. Hava, Goodword Books, 81-87570-69-5, pb.

**The Basic Concepts in the Quran,** Harun Yahya, Goodword Books, 81-87570-02-4, pb.

**A Basic Dictionary of Islam**, Ruqaiyyah Waris Maqsood, Goodword Books, 81-85063-30-3, pb.

**The Blessings of Ramadan**, Javed Ali, Goodword Books, 81-87570-10-9, pb.

**A Brief Illustrated Guide to Understanding Islam**, I.A. Ibrahim, Goodword Books, 81-7898-072-X, pb.

**The Call of the Quran**, Maulana Wahiduddin Khan, Goodword Books, 81-87570-03-2, pb.

## Suggestions for Reading

**The Essential Arabic**, Rafi'el-Imad Faynan, Goodword Books, 81-85063-26-5, pb.

**The Essential Koran: The Heart of Islam,** Translated and presented by Thomas Cleary, Book Sales, 1998. D-7858-09023, hb. The author has selected passages that, in his opinion, best lead the non-Muslim to understanding.

**Ever Thought About the Truth?**, Harun Yahya, Goodword Books, 81-87570-15-6, pb.

**Examining Religions: Islam**, Rosalyn Kendrick, Heinemann Educational, 0-435-30314-7, pb.

**From the Lives of the Khulafa' Ar-Rashidun**, Huseyin Abiva, IQRA' International Educational Foundation, 1-56316-379-9, pb.

**God Arises**, Maulana Wahiduddin Khan, Goodword Books, 81-85063-14-1, pb.

**Goodword Islamic Studies Grades 1-6**, Saniyasnain Khan, Goodword Books, 81-7898-052-5, pb.

**The Junior Dictionary of Islam,** Saniyasnain Khan, Goodword Books, 81-87570-74-1, pb.

**The Greatest Stories from the Quran**, Saniyasnain Khan, Goodword Books, 81-7898-097-5, hb.

**A Guide for the Young Muslims (Book One)**, Assad Nimer Busool, Goodword Books, 81-7898-055-X, pb.

**A Guide for the Young Muslims (Book Two)**, Assad Nimer Busool, Goodword Books, 81-7898-056-8, pb.

## Suggestions for Reading

**A Guide for the Young Muslims (Book Four)**, Assad Nimer Busool, Goodword Books, 81-7898-064-9, pb.

**The Hadith for Beginners**, Dr. Muhammad Zubayr Siddiqui, Goodword Books, 81-87570-16-4, pb.

**A Handbook of Muslim Belief**, Dr. Ahmad A. Galwash, Goodword Books, 81-87570-46-6, pb.

**The Handy Concordance of the Quran**, Aurang Zeb Azmi, Goodword Books, 81-7898-093-2, pb.

**The Holy Quran**, Tr. by Abdullah Yusuf Ali, Goodword Books, 81-87570-39-3, pb; 81-7898-002-9, hb.

**The Holy Qur'an: Text, Translation and Commentary.** Abdullah Yusuf Ali. 1987, IPCI: Islamic Vision, Birmingham, pb. A standard English version, with extensive notes.

**I'm Learning About Eid-ul-Fitr,** Saniyasnain Khan, Goodword Books, 81-7898-065-7, hb/pb.

**I'm Learning About the Prophet Muhammad,** Saniyasnain Khan, Goodword Books, 81-7898-086-X, pb; 81-7898-082-7, hb.

**Introducing Islam**, Maulana Wahiduddin Khan, Goodword Books, 81-87570-58-X, pb.

**Islam: An Introduction,** Annemarie Schimmel, 1992, State University of New York Press, 0-7914-1328-4, pb. A lifelong scholar's clear, insightful and reliable overview of the faith.

**Islam: A Primer.** John Sabic, 6th ex. 2001, AMIDEAST, 0-913957-17-8, pb. An easy-to-read, no-frills field guide to Islam's origins and beliefs, with notes on social customs and rituals such as hospitality, weddings and births.

**Islam: Creator of the Modern Age**, Maulana Wahiduddin Khan, Goodword Books, 81-87570-30-X, pb.

**Islam: Beliefs and Teachings**, Ghulam Sarwar, The Muslim Educational Trust, 0-907261-03-5, pb.

**Islam: A Short History,** Karen Armstrong, 2000, Modern Library, 0-679-64040-1, hb. One of the best books on the shelf for non-Muslims who want to lay the foundation for a factual, sensibly panoramic understanding of Islam.

**Islam: The Voice of Human Nature**, Maulana Wahiduddin Khan, Goodword Books, 81-87570-29-6, pb.

**Islam and Peace**, Maulana Wahiduddin Khan, Goodword Books, 81-87570-28-8, pb.

**Islam As It Is**, Maulana Wahiduddin Khan, Goodword Books, 81-87570-66-0, pb.

**Islam in America.** Jane I. Smith. 1999, Columbia University Press, 0-231-10967-9, pb. An excellent panoramic view of the Muslim experience in America.

**Islam the Natural Way**, Abdul Wahid Hamid, Muslim Education and Literary Services, 0-948196-09-2, pb.

**Islam Rediscovered**, Maulana Wahiduddin Khan, Goodword Books, 81-87570-40-7, pb.

**The Islamic Art and Architecture**, Prof. T.W. Arnold, Goodword Books, 81-87570-52-0, pb.

## Suggestions for Reading

**An Islamic Treasury of Virtues**, Maulana Wahiduddin Khan, Goodword Books, 81-85063-97-4, pb.

**Learn The Arabic Alphabet Through the Beautiful Names of Allah**, Assad Nimer Busool, Goodword Books, 81-7898-054-1, pb.

**The Life of the Last Prophet,** Yusuf Islam, Mountain of Light, 1-900675-00-5, hb.

**The Light of Dawn: A Daybook of Verses from the Holy Qur'an.** Selected and rendered by Camille Adams Helminski. 1998, Shambhala, 0-939660-60-1, hb. An assemblage of verses from all 114 chapters of the Qur'an offers a gateway to the spiritual depth of Islam.

**Living Islam: Treading the Path of Ideal**, Ruqaiyyah Waris Maqsood, Goodword Books, 81-85063-27-3, pb.

**The Meaning of the Glorious Koran.** Mohammed Marmaduke Pickthall. 1996, Amana, 0-915957-22-1, hb. An English rendering of the Holy Book, justifiably famous for the beauty and sensitivity of the language.

**The Miracle in the Ant**, Harun Yahya, Goodword Books, 81-87570-13-X, pb.

**The Miracle of Creation in Plants**, Harun Yahya, Goodword Books, 81-7898-017-7, pb.

**The Moral Values of the Quran**, Harun Yahya, Goodword Books, 81-87570-27-X, pb.

**The Moral Vision**, Maulana Wahiduddin Khan, Goodword Books, 81-87570-01-6, pb.

## Suggestions for Reading

**The Most Beautiful Names of Allah**, Samira Fayyad Khawaldeh, Goodword Books, 81-7898-016-9, pb; 81-7898-005-3, hb.

**Muhammad: A Biography of the Prophet.** Karen Armstrong. 1993, Harper Collins, 0-06-250886-5, pb; 0-06-250014-7, hb. A respected western scholar provides a readable and sympathetic account of Muhammad's life, including contextual information about economics and politics of his time.

**Muhammad: A Prophet for All Humanity**, Maulana Wahiduddin Khan, Goodword Books, 81-85063-84-2, pb.

**Muhammad: His Life Based on the Earliest Sources.** Martin Lings.1987, Inner Traditions International, Ltd., 0-89281-170-6, pb. A well-narrated biography by a British Muslim scholar, based on traditional sources.

**Muslim Marriage Guide**, Ruqaiyyah Waris Maqsood, Goodword Books, 81-85063-25-7, pb.

**The Muslim Prayer Encyclopaedia**, Ruqaiyyah Waris Maqsood, Goodword Books, 81-85063-29-X, pb.

**One Religion**, Zaheer U. Ahmed, Goodword Books, 81-87570-47-4, pb.

**One Thousand Roads to Mecca: Ten Centuries of Travellers Writing about the Muslim Pilgrimage.** Michael Wolfe, ed. grove, 0-8021-3599-4, pb. Accounts by 23 pilgrims of a dozen nationalities who made their ways to Makkah between 1150 and 1990 illuminate the Hajj and Islam.

## Suggestions for Reading

**The Oxford History of Islam.** John L. Esposito. 2000, Oxford, 0-19-510799-3, hb. An excellent resource in terms of breadth, edited by a thoughtful and well-regarded American scholar of Islam.

**The Pilgrimage to Makkah**, Sir Richard F. Burton, Goodword Books, 81-87570-73-3, pb.

**Prayers of the Last Prophet,** Yusuf Islam, Mountain of Light, 1-900675-05-6, hb.

**Presenting the Quran**, Saniyasnain Khan, Goodword Books, 81-85063-95-8, pb.

**Principles of Islam**, Maulana Wahiduddin Khan, Goodword Books, 81-85063-36-2, pb.

**The Prophet Muhammad: A Simple Guide to His Life,** Maulana Wahiduddin Khan, Goodword Books, 81-7898-094-0, pb.

**Quick Grasp of Faith**, Harun Yahya, Goodword Books, 81-87570-17-2, pb.

**The Quran: An Abiding Wonder,** Maulana Wahiduddin Khan, Goodword Books, 81-85063-68-0, pb.

**Quran Stories for Kids,** Saniyasnain Khan, Goodword Books, 81-7898-099-1, hb.

**Quran Stories for Little Hearts**, Saniyasnain Khan, Goodword Books, a set of 12 books, hb/pb.

**The Road to Makkah.** Muhammad Asad. 2001, Fons Vitae, 1-887752-37-4, pb; 1999, Islamic Book Trust, 983-9154-12-5, hb. A fascinating and moving spiritual

## Suggestions for Reading

autobiography of a sophisticated westerner's journey into Islam.

**A Simple Guide to Islam**, Farida Khanam, Goodword Books, 81-87570-71-7, pb.

**A Simple Guide to Islam's Contribution to Science**, Maulvi Abdul Karim, Goodword Books, 81-87570-45-8, pb.

**A Simple Guide to Muslim Prayer,** Muhammad Mahmud Al-Sawwat, Goodword Books, 81-87570-26-1, pb.

**A Simple Guide to the Recitation of the Quran**, Syed Mahmood Hasan, Goodword Books, 81-7898-095-9, pb.

**The Spread of Islam in the World**, Prof. Thomas Arnold, Goodword Books, 81-87570-22-9, pb.

**The Story of Islamic Spain**, Syed Azizur Rahman, Goodword Books, 81-87570-57-1, pb.

**The Soul of the Quran**, Saniyasnain Khan, Goodword Books, 81-85063-13-3, pb.

**Tell Me About Hajj**, Saniyasnain Khan, Goodword Books, 81-87570-90-3, pb; 81-87570-00-8, hb.

**Tell Me About the Prophet Muhammad**, Saniyasnain Khan, Goodword Books, 81-87570-11-3, hb.

**Tell Me About the Prophet Musa**, Saniyasnain Khan, Goodword Books, 81-87570-48-2, hb.

**Tell Me About the Prophet Yusuf**, Saniyasnain Khan, Goodword Books, 81-87570-64-4, hb.

## Suggestions for Reading

**Those Promised Paradise**, Noura Durkee, IQRA' International Educational Foundation, 1-56316-374-8, pb.

**The True Jihad**, Maulana Wahiduddin Khan, 81-7898-068-1, hb.

**Understanding Islam and the Muslims.** 1990, The Islamic Texts Society, 0-946-62120-9, pb. An illustrated question-and-answer guide to basic beliefs. Excellent for discussion groups.

**What Everyone Should Know about Islam and Muslims.** Suzanne Haneef. 1995, Library of Islam, 0-935782-00-1, pb. A clear guide to basic tenets and their expression in beliefs, worship, festivals, values and standards of conduct.

**Windows on the House of Islam: Muslim Sources on Spirituality and Religious Life.** John Renard, ed.1998, University of California Press, 0-520-20976-1, hb; 0-520-21086-7, pb. A collection from more than 30 classical and modern writers and artists to help non-Muslims fathom what it means to be a Muslim.

**Woman in Islamic Shariah**, Maulana Wahiduddin Khan, Goodword Books, 81-87570-31-8, pb.

# Prayers from the Quran

$$\text{بِسْمِ ٱللَّهِ ٱلرَّحْمَٰنِ ٱلرَّحِيمِ}$$
$$\text{ٱلْحَمْدُ لِلَّهِ رَبِّ ٱلْعَٰلَمِينَ ۝ ٱلرَّحْمَٰنِ ٱلرَّحِيمِ ۝ مَٰلِكِ يَوْمِ ٱلدِّينِ ۝}$$
$$\text{إِيَّاكَ نَعْبُدُ وَإِيَّاكَ نَسْتَعِينُ ۝ ٱهْدِنَا ٱلصِّرَٰطَ ٱلْمُسْتَقِيمَ ۝}$$
$$\text{صِرَٰطَ ٱلَّذِينَ أَنْعَمْتَ عَلَيْهِمْ غَيْرِ ٱلْمَغْضُوبِ عَلَيْهِمْ وَلَا ٱلضَّآلِّينَ ۝}$$

Praise to Allah, Lord of the Universe, the Beneficent, the Merciful, Master of the Day of Judgement. You alone we worship, and to You alone we turn for help. Guide us to the straight path. The path of those who have found Your favour, not of those who have incurred Your wrath, nor of those who have gone astray. (1:1-7)

$$\text{وَقُل رَّبِّ زِدْنِى عِلْمًا ۝}$$

Lord, increase my knowledge. (20:114)

$$\text{رَبَّنَا ظَلَمْنَآ أَنفُسَنَا وَإِن لَّمْ تَغْفِرْ لَنَا وَتَرْحَمْنَا لَنَكُونَنَّ مِنَ ٱلْخَٰسِرِينَ ۝}$$

Lord, we have wronged our souls. Pardon us and have mercy on us, or we shall surely be among the lost. (7:23)

$$\text{أَنِّى مَغْلُوبٌ فَٱنتَصِرْ ۝}$$

Help me, Lord, I am overcome! (54:10)

## Prayers from the Quran

$$رَبَّنَآ أَفْرِغْ عَلَيْنَا صَبْرًا وَتَوَفَّنَا مُسْلِمِينَ ۝$$

Lord, give us patience and let us die in submission. (7:126)

$$رَبِّ إِنِّي لِمَآ أَنزَلْتَ إِلَيَّ مِنْ خَيْرٍ فَقِيرٌ ۝$$

Lord, I stand in dire need of any good which You may bestow upon me! (28:24)

$$رَبَّنَآ ءَامَنَّا فَٱغْفِرْ لَنَا وَٱرْحَمْنَا وَأَنتَ خَيْرُ ٱلرَّٰحِمِينَ ۝$$

Our lord, we believe; therefore forgive us, and have mercy on us, for You are the best of the merciful. (23:109)

$$رَّبِّ أَعُوذُ بِكَ مِنْ هَمَزَٰتِ ٱلشَّيَٰطِينِ ۝ وَأَعُوذُ بِكَ رَبِّ أَن يَحْضُرُونِ ۝$$

Lord, I seek refuge in You from the promptings of all evil impulses. Lord, I seek refuge with You from their presence. (23:98-99)

$$رَبِّ إِنِّي ظَلَمْتُ نَفْسِي فَٱغْفِرْ لِي ۝$$

My Lord, Forgive me! for I have sinned against my soul. (28:16)

$$رَبَّنَآ ءَاتِنَا مِن لَّدُنكَ رَحْمَةً وَهَيِّئْ لَنَا مِنْ أَمْرِنَا رَشَدًا ۝$$

Our Lord! Send upon us Your mercy, and show us the solution to our problem in the right way. (18:10)

**Prayers from the Quran**

$$\text{إِنَّ صَلَاتِي وَنُسُكِي وَمَحْيَايَ وَمَمَاتِي لِلَّهِ رَبِّ ٱلْعَٰلَمِينَ}$$

Say 'My prayer, my worship, my living, my dying are for Allah alone, the lord of all Being.' (6:162)

$$\text{رَبَّنَآ ءَامَنَّا بِمَآ أَنزَلْتَ وَٱتَّبَعْنَا ٱلرَّسُولَ فَٱكْتُبْنَا مَعَ ٱلشَّٰهِدِينَ}$$

Our Lord! We believe in what You have revealed, and we follow the Messenger; so write us down among those who bear witness. (3:53)

$$\text{رَبَّنَا ٱغْفِرْ لَنَا وَلِإِخْوَٰنِنَا ٱلَّذِينَ سَبَقُونَا بِٱلْإِيمَٰنِ وَلَا تَجْعَلْ فِي قُلُوبِنَا غِلًّا لِّلَّذِينَ ءَامَنُوا۟ رَبَّنَآ إِنَّكَ رَءُوفٌ رَّحِيمٌ}$$

Forgive us Lord, and forgive our brothers who embraced the Faith before us. Do not put in our hearts any malice towards the faithful. Lord, You are Compassionate and Merciful. (59:10)

$$\text{أَنتَ وَلِيُّنَا فَٱغْفِرْ لَنَا وَٱرْحَمْنَا وَأَنتَ خَيْرُ ٱلْغَٰفِرِينَ وَٱكْتُبْ لَنَا فِي هَٰذِهِ ٱلدُّنْيَا حَسَنَةً وَفِي ٱلْءَاخِرَةِ إِنَّا هُدْنَآ إِلَيْكَ}$$

Lord, You alone are our Guardian. Forgive us and have mercy on us: You are the noblest of those who forgive. Ordain for us what is good, both in this life and in the Hereafter. To You alone we turn. (7:155-156)

**Prayers from the Quran**

$$\text{رَبَّنَا هَبْ لَنَا مِنْ أَزْوَاجِنَا وَذُرِّيَّاتِنَا قُرَّةَ أَعْيُنٍ وَاجْعَلْنَا لِلْمُتَّقِينَ إِمَامًا}$$

Lord, give us joy in our spouses and children and make us foremost among those who are conscious of You. (25: 74)

$$\text{سُبْحَانَ الَّذِي سَخَّرَ لَنَا هَذَا وَمَا كُنَّا لَهُ مُقْرِنِينَ وَإِنَّا إِلَى رَبِّنَا لَمُنقَلِبُونَ}$$

Glory to be to Him, who has subjected these to us. We ourselves were not able to subdue them. To our Lord we shall all return. (43:13-14)

$$\text{رَبِّ أَدْخِلْنِي مُدْخَلَ صِدْقٍ وَأَخْرِجْنِي مُخْرَجَ صِدْقٍ وَاجْعَل لِّي مِن لَّدُنكَ سُلْطَانًا نَّصِيرًا}$$

Lord, grant me a goodly entrance and a goodly exit, and sustain me with Your power. (17:80)

$$\text{رَبَّنَا اغْفِرْ لَنَا ذُنُوبَنَا وَإِسْرَافَنَا فِي أَمْرِنَا وَثَبِّتْ أَقْدَامَنَا وَانصُرْنَا عَلَى الْقَوْمِ الْكَافِرِينَ}$$

Our Lord! Forgive us our sins and the lack of moderation in our doings. Make our steps firm, and help us against those who deny the faith. (3:147)

**Prayers from the Quran**

رَبِّ أَوْزِعْنِي أَنْ أَشْكُرَ نِعْمَتَكَ ٱلَّتِي أَنْعَمْتَ عَلَيَّ وَعَلَىٰ وَٰلِدَيَّ وَأَنْ أَعْمَلَ صَٰلِحًا تَرْضَىٰهُ وَأَدْخِلْنِي بِرَحْمَتِكَ فِي عِبَادِكَ ٱلصَّٰلِحِينَ ۝

Inspire me, Lord, that I may forever be grateful for the blessings You have bestowed on me and on my parents, and that I may do good works that will please You and include me through Your mercy amongst Your righteous servants. (27:19)

ٱللَّهُمَّ مَٰلِكَ ٱلْمُلْكِ تُؤْتِي ٱلْمُلْكَ مَن تَشَآءُ وَتَنزِعُ ٱلْمُلْكَ مِمَّن تَشَآءُ وَتُعِزُّ مَن تَشَآءُ وَتُذِلُّ مَن تَشَآءُ بِيَدِكَ ٱلْخَيْرُ إِنَّكَ عَلَىٰ كُلِّ شَىْءٍ قَدِيرٌ ۝ تُولِجُ ٱلَّيْلَ فِي ٱلنَّهَارِ وَتُولِجُ ٱلنَّهَارَ فِي ٱلَّيْلِ وَتُخْرِجُ ٱلْحَىَّ مِنَ ٱلْمَيِّتِ وَتُخْرِجُ ٱلْمَيِّتَ مِنَ ٱلْحَىِّ وَتَرْزُقُ مَن تَشَآءُ بِغَيْرِ حِسَابٍ ۝

Lord, Sovereign of all sovereignty, You bestow power on whom You will and take it away from whom You please; You exalt whoever You will and abase whoever You please. In Your hand lies all that is good; You have power over all things. You cause the night to pass into the day and the day into the night; You bring forth the living from the dead and the dead from the living. You give without measure to whom You will. (3:26-27 )

**Prayers from the Quran**

رَبَّنَا لَا تُزِغْ قُلُوبَنَا بَعْدَ إِذْ هَدَيْتَنَا وَهَبْ لَنَا مِن لَّدُنكَ رَحْمَةً إِنَّكَ أَنتَ ٱلْوَهَّابُ ۞ رَبَّنَا إِنَّكَ جَامِعُ ٱلنَّاسِ لِيَوْمٍ لَّا رَيْبَ فِيهِ إِنَّ ٱللَّهَ لَا يُخْلِفُ ٱلْمِيعَادَ ۞

Our Lord, do not cause our hearts to go astray after You have guided us. Grant us Your own mercy; You are the generous Giver. Lord, You will surely gather all humanity before You upon a day that will indubitably come. Allah will not break His promise. (3:8-9)

رَبَّنَا لَا تُؤَاخِذْنَا إِن نَّسِينَا أَوْ أَخْطَأْنَا رَبَّنَا وَلَا تَحْمِلْ عَلَيْنَا إِصْرًا كَمَا حَمَلْتَهُ عَلَى ٱلَّذِينَ مِن قَبْلِنَا رَبَّنَا وَلَا تُحَمِّلْنَا مَا لَا طَاقَةَ لَنَا بِهِ وَٱعْفُ عَنَّا وَٱغْفِرْ لَنَا وَٱرْحَمْنَا أَنتَ مَوْلَىٰنَا فَٱنصُرْنَا عَلَى ٱلْقَوْمِ ٱلْكَافِرِينَ ۞

Our Lord, take us not to task if we forget, or lapse into error. Our Lord, charge us not with the burden You laid upon those before us. Our Lord, do not burden us beyond what we have the strength to bear. And pardon us, and forgive us our sins, and have mercy on us, You alone are our Protector. And help us against people who deny the truth. (2:286)

**Prayers from the Quran**

$$رَبِّ ٱشْرَحْ لِى صَدْرِى ۝ وَيَسِّرْ لِىٓ أَمْرِى ۝$$
$$وَٱحْلُلْ عُقْدَةً مِّن لِّسَانِى ۝ يَفْقَهُوا۟ قَوْلِى ۝$$

Lord, put courage into my heart, and ease my task for me. Free the knot of my tongue, that they may understand my message. (20:25-28)

$$رَبَّنَا مَا خَلَقْتَ هَـٰذَا بَـٰطِلًا سُبْحَـٰنَكَ فَقِنَا عَذَابَ ٱلنَّارِ ۝$$
$$رَبَّنَآ إِنَّكَ مَن تُدْخِلِ ٱلنَّارَ فَقَدْ أَخْزَيْتَهُۥ ۖ وَمَا لِلظَّـٰلِمِينَ مِنْ أَنصَارٍ ۝$$
$$رَّبَّنَآ إِنَّنَا سَمِعْنَا مُنَادِيًا يُنَادِى لِلْإِيمَـٰنِ أَنْ ءَامِنُوا۟ بِرَبِّكُمْ فَـَٔامَنَّا ۚ$$
$$رَبَّنَا فَٱغْفِرْ لَنَا ذُنُوبَنَا وَكَفِّرْ عَنَّا سَيِّـَٔاتِنَا وَتَوَفَّنَا مَعَ ٱلْأَبْرَارِ ۝$$
$$رَبَّنَا وَءَاتِنَا مَا وَعَدتَّنَا عَلَىٰ رُسُلِكَ وَلَا تُخْزِنَا يَوْمَ ٱلْقِيَـٰمَةِ ۗ إِنَّكَ لَا تُخْلِفُ ٱلْمِيعَادَ ۝$$

'Our Lord You have not created this (universe) in vain. Glory be to You! Save us from the suffering of the Fire. Our Lord, those whom You will cast into the Fire, You will put to eternal shame; and the evildoers shall have no helpers. Our Lord, we have heard the call of one calling us to the true faith, saying, "Believe in the Lord!" And we believed. Our Lord, forgive us our sins and remove from us our bad deeds, and take our souls to Yourself with the righteous. Our Lord, grant us what You have promised us through Your Messengers, and save us from disgrace on the Day of Resurrection; You will never break Your promise!'(3:190-194)

### Prayers from the Quran

رَبِّ أَوْزِعْنِي أَنْ أَشْكُرَ نِعْمَتَكَ الَّتِي أَنْعَمْتَ عَلَيَّ وَعَلَىٰ وَالِدَيَّ وَأَنْ أَعْمَلَ صَالِحًا تَرْضَاهُ وَأَصْلِحْ لِي فِي ذُرِّيَّتِي إِنِّي تُبْتُ إِلَيْكَ وَإِنِّي مِنَ الْمُسْلِمِينَ ۝

Inspire me, my Lord that I may be thankful for Your blessing bestowed on me and my parents, and that I may do good works that will please You. Grant me good descendants. To You I turn and to You I surrender myself. (46:15)

# Prayers from the Hadith

يَا مُقَلِّبَ الْقُلُوْبِ ثَبِّتْ قَلْبِى عَلىٰ دِيْنِكَ ⃝

O Turner of the hearts, make my heart firm upon Your religion.
(Related by al-Tirmidhi, Ahmad and al-Haakim.)

اَللَّهُمَّ إِنِّى أَسْأَلُكَ الْهُدَىٰ، وَالتُّقَىٰ، وَالْعَفَافَ وَالْغِنىٰ ⃝

O Allah, I ask You for guidance, piety, uprightness and prosperity. (Related by Muslim.)

اللَّهُمَّ مُصَرِّفَ الْقُلُوْبِ صَرِّفْ قُلُوْبَنَا عَلىٰ طَاعَتِكَ ⃝

O Allah, the turner of the hearts, set our hearts upon obedience to You. (Related by Muslim.)

اللَّهُمَّ إِنِّى أَسْأَلُكَ الْعَافِيَةَ فِى الدُّنْيَا وَالآخِرَةِ ⃝

Allah, I ask You for well-being in this life and the Hereafter. (Related by al-Tirmidhi.)

اَللَّهُمَّ اهْدِنِى وَسَدِّدْنِى، اللَهُمَّ إِنِّى أَسْأَلُكَ الْهُدىٰ وَالسَّدَادَ ⃝

O Allah, guide me and keep me to what is right. O Allah, I ask You for guidance and to keep me on the right path. (Related by Muslim.)

**Prayers from the Hadith**

$$\text{اللَّهُمَّ إِنِّى أَعُوذُبِكَ مِنْ شَرِّ مَا عَمِلْتُ، ومِنْ شَرِّ مَا لَمْ أَعْمَلْ}$$

O Allah, I seek refuge in You from the evil which I have done and the evil which I have not done. (Related by Muslim.)

$$\text{اللَّهُمَّ إِنِّىْ أَعُوذُ بِكَ مِنْ زَوَالِ نِعْمَتِكَ، وَتَحَوُّلِ عَافِيَتِكَ، وَفُجَاءَةِ نَقْمَتِكَ، وجَمِيْعِ سَخَطِكَ}$$

O Allah, I seek refuge in You from the absence of Your favours, a change in Your granting me well-being, a sudden vengeance wrought by You and all that displeases You. (Related by Muslim.)

$$\text{اللَّهُمَّ أَكْثِرْ مَا لِى، وَوَلَدِىْ، وَبَارِكْ لِىْ فِيْمَا أَعْطَيْتَنِى وَأَطِلْ حَيَاتِىْ عَلَى طَاعَتِكَ وَأَحْسِنْ عَمَلِىْ وَاغْفِرْلِىْ}$$

O Allah, increase my wealth, my children and bless me in what You have granted me. Make my life longer upon your obedience, make my deeds the best and forgive me. (Related by al-Bukhari and Muslim.)

## Prayers from the Hadith

اللَّهُمَّ رَحْمَتَكَ أَرْجُو فَلَا تَكِلْنِى إِلَىٰ نَفْسِي طَرْفَةَ عَيْنٍ، وَأَصْلِحْ لِى شَأْنِي كُلَّهُ، لَا إِلٰهَ إِلاَّ أَنْتَ O

O Allah, I hope for Your mercy, so do not leave me to myself even for an instant. Set all of my affairs in order. There is no deity which has the right to be worshipped except You alone.
(Related by Abu Da'ud and Ahmad.)

لَا إِلٰهَ إِلاَّ اللهُ الْعَظِيْمُ الْحَلِيْمُ، لَا إِلٰهَ إِلاَّ اللهُ رَبُّ الْعَرْشِ الْعَظِيْمِ، لَا إِلٰهَ إِلاَّ اللهُ رَبُّ السَّمٰوَاتِ، وَرَبُّ الْأَرْضِ، وَرَبُّ الْعَرْشِ الْكَرِيْمِ O

There is no deity which has the right to be worshipped except Allah alone, the Mighty, the Wise.
There is no deity which has the right to be worshipped except Allah alone, Lord of the Mighty throne.
There is no deity which has the right to be worshipped except Allah alone, Lord of the Heavens, the earth and the Noble Throne.
(Related by al-Bukhari and Muslim.)

## Prayers from the Hadith

اللَّهُمَّ أَصْلِحْ لِيْ دِيْنِيَ الَّذِي هُوَ عِصْمَةُ أَمْرِيْ، وَأَصْلِحْ لِيْ دُنْيَايَ الَّتِي فِيْهَا مَعَاشِيْ، وَأَصْلِحْ لِيْ آخِرَتِي الَّتِي فِيْهَا مَعَادِيْ، وَاجْعَلِ الْحَيَاةَ زِيَادَةً لِّيْ فِيْ كُلِّ خَيْرٍ، وَاجْعَلِ الْمَوْتَ رَاحَةً لِّيْ مِنْ كُلِّ شَرٍّ ۞

O Allah, put my religion in order for me, which is the basis of my affairs. Put in order for me my worldly affairs which are the source of my livelihood. Put in order for me my life in the Hereafter, which is my ultimate destination. Increase all that is good in my life and make death a respite for me from every evil. (Related by Muslim.)

اللَّهُمَّ إِنِّي أَعُوْذُبِكَ مِنَ الْعَجْزِ، وَالْكَسْلِ، وَالْجُبْنِ، وَالْبُخْلِ، وَالْهَرَمِ وَعَذَابِ الْقَبْرِ، اللَّهُمَّ آتِ نَفْسِي تَقْوَاهَا، وَزَكِّهَا أَنْتَ خَيْرُ مَنْ زَكَّاهَا. أَنْتَ وَلِيُّهَا وَمَوْلَاهَا. اللَّهُمَّ إِنِّي أَعُوْذُ بِكَ مِنْ عِلْمٍ لَا يَنْفَعُ، وَمِنْ قَلْبٍ لَّا يَخْشَعُ، وَمِنْ نَفْسٍ لَّا تَشْبَعُ، وَمِنْ دَعْوَةٍ لَّا يُسْتَجَابُ لَهَا ۞

O Allah, I seek refuge in You from weakness, laziness, cowardliness, meanness, senility and the punishment of the grave. O Allah, give my soul sufficient piety to fear You, and purify it, as You are the best one who can

**Prayers from the Hadith**

purify it. You are its Patron and Master. O Allah, I seek refuge in You from knowledge which is of no benefit, a heart which has no fear, an appetite which is insatiable and a supplication which is not answered.
(Related by Muslim.)

اللَّهُمَّ إِنِّى عَبْدُكَ ابْنُ عَبْدِكَ، ابْنُ أَمَتِكَ، نَاصِيَتِى بِيَدِكَ، مَاضٍ فِىَّ حُكْمُكَ، عَدْلٌ فِىَّ قَضَاؤُكَ. أَسْأَلُكَ بِكُلِّ اسْمٍ هُوَ لَكَ سَمَّيْتَ بِهِ نَفْسَكَ، أَوْ أَنْزَلْتَهُ فِى كِتَابِكَ، أَوْ عَلَّمْتَهُ أَحَداً مِنْ خَلْقِكَ، أَوِ اسْتَأْثَرْتَ بِهِ فِى عِلْمِ الْغَيْبِ عِنْدَكَ، أَنْ تَجْعَلَ الْقُرْآنَ رَبِيعَ قَلْبِىْ، وَنُوْرَ صَدْرِىْ، وَجَلَاءَ حُزْنِى، وَذَهَابَ هَمِّىْ ۝

O Allah, indeed I am Your servant, the son of Your servant and the son of Your female servant. I am under the control of Your Hand. Your Judgement on me shall come to pass and Your Judgement on me is just. I ask of You by all the Names by which You have named Yourself, or revealed in Your book, or taught to any of Your creation, or You have kept hidden in the matters of the unseen with You: Make the Qur'an the spring of my heart and the light of my life. Take away my sorrow and my worries.
(Related by Ahmad and al-Haakim.)

# Important Phrases

Masha Allah مَاشَاءَ اللّٰهُ

Allah has willed it.

Insha Allah اِنْ شَاءَ اللّٰهُ

If Allah wills.

Astaghfirullah اَسْتَغْفِرُ اللّٰهَ

I seek Allah's forgiveness.

A'udhubillah اَعُوْذُ بِاللّٰهِ

I seek refuge in Allah.

Jazak-Allah جَزَاكَ اللّٰهُ

May Allah reward you.

Al-hamdulillah اَلْحَمْدُ لِلّٰهِ

Praise be to Allah.

# Surah Al-Fatiha
## THE OPENING

سُورَةُ الْفَاتِحَةِ

بِسْمِ اللهِ الرَّحْمٰنِ الرَّحِيْمِ

اَلْحَمْدُ لِلّٰهِ رَبِّ الْعٰلَمِيْنَ ۞ الرَّحْمٰنِ الرَّحِيْمِ ۞ مٰلِكِ يَوْمِ الدِّيْنِ ۞ اِيَّاكَ نَعْبُدُ وَاِيَّاكَ نَسْتَعِيْنُ ۞ اِهْدِنَا الصِّرَاطَ الْمُسْتَقِيْمَ ۞ صِرَاطَ الَّذِيْنَ اَنْعَمْتَ عَلَيْهِمْ ۞ غَيْرِ الْمَغْضُوْبِ عَلَيْهِمْ وَلَا الضَّآلِّيْنَ ۞

In the name of Allah,
the Compassionate, the Merciful.

Praise be to Allah, Lord of the Universe,
the Compassionate, the Merciful,
Master of the Day of Judgement.
You alone we worship, and to You alone
we turn for help. Guide us to the straight path,
the path of those whom You have favoured,
not of those who have incurred Your wrath,
nor of those who have gone astray.

# Surah Al-Kausar
**ABUNDANCE**

سُوْرَةُ الْكَوْثَرِ

بِسْمِ اللهِ الرَّحْمٰنِ الرَّحِيْمِ

اِنَّآ اَعْطَيْنٰكَ الْكَوْثَرَ ۞

فَصَلِّ لِرَبِّكَ وَانْحَرْ ۞

اِنَّ شَانِئَكَ هُوَ الْاَبْتَرُ ۞

In the name of Allah,
the Compassionate, the Merciful.

We have given you abundance.
Pray to your Lord and sacrifice to Him.
He that hates you shall remain childless.

# Surah Al-Kafirun
## THE UNBELIEVERS

سُوْرَةُ الْكٰفِرُوْنَ

بِسْمِ اللهِ الرَّحْمٰنِ الرَّحِيْمِ

قُلْ يٰٓاَيُّهَا الْكٰفِرُوْنَ ۙ لَآ اَعْبُدُ مَا تَعْبُدُوْنَ ۙ وَلَآ اَنْتُمْ عٰبِدُوْنَ مَآ اَعْبُدُ ۚ وَلَآ اَنَا عَابِدٌ مَّا عَبَدْتُّمْ ۙ وَلَآ اَنْتُمْ عٰبِدُوْنَ مَآ اَعْبُدُ ۭ لَكُمْ دِيْنُكُمْ وَلِيَ دِيْنِ ۧ

In the name of Allah,
the Compassionate, the Merciful.

Say: "Unbelievers, I do not worship what you worship, nor do you worship what I worship. I shall never worship what you worship. Nor will you ever worship what I worship. You have your own religion, and I have mine.'

# Surah Al-Nasr

**HELP**

سُوْرَةُ النَّصْرِ

بِسْمِ اللهِ الرَّحْمٰنِ الرَّحِيْمِ

إِذَا جَآءَ نَصْرُ اللهِ وَالْفَتْحُ ۞

وَرَأَيْتَ النَّاسَ يَدْخُلُوْنَ فِيْ دِيْنِ اللهِ أَفْوَاجًا ۞

فَسَبِّحْ بِحَمْدِ رَبِّكَ وَاسْتَغْفِرْهُ ۚ إِنَّهٗ كَانَ تَوَّابًا ۞

In the name of Allah,
the Compassionate, the Merciful.

When God's help and victory come, and you see men embrace God's faith in multitudes, gives glory to your Lord and seek His pardon. He is ever disposed to mercy.

# Surah Al-Lahab
**THE FLAME**

سُورَةُ اللَّهَبِ

بِسْمِ اللهِ الرَّحْمٰنِ الرَّحِيْمِ

تَبَّتْ يَدَآ أَبِىْ لَهَبٍ وَّتَبَّ ۚ

مَآ أَغْنٰى عَنْهُ مَالُهُ وَمَا كَسَبَ ۚ

سَيَصْلٰى نَارًا ذَاتَ لَهَبٍ ۚ

وَّامْرَأَتُهٗ ۚ حَمَّالَةَ الْحَطَبِ ۚ

فِىْ جِيْدِهَا حَبْلٌ مِّنْ مَّسَدٍ ۚ

In the name of Allah,
the Compassionate, the Merciful.

May the hands of Abu-Lahab perish! May he himself perish! Nothing shall his wealth and gains avail him. He shall be burnt in a flaming fire, and his wife, laden with Faggots, shall have a rope of fibre round her neck!

# Surah Al-Ikhlas

**ONENESS**

سُوْرَةُ الْاِخْلَاصِ

بِسْمِ اللهِ الرَّحْمٰنِ الرَّحِيْمِ

قُلْ هُوَ اللهُ اَحَدٌ ۚ اَللهُ الصَّمَدُ ۚ
لَمْ يَلِدْ ۙ وَلَمْ يُوْلَدْ ۙ
وَلَمْ يَكُنْ لَّهٗ كُفُوًا اَحَدٌ ۚ

In the name of Allah,
the Compassionate, the Merciful.

Say: God is One, the Eternal God.
He begot none, nor was He begotten.
None is equal to Him.

# Surah Al-Falaq

**DAYBREAK**

سُوْرَةُ الْفَلَقِ

بِسْمِ اللهِ الرَّحْمٰنِ الرَّحِيْمِ

قُلْ اَعُوْذُ بِرَبِّ الْفَلَقِ ۞ مِنْ شَرِّ مَا خَلَقَ ۞
وَمِنْ شَرِّ غَاسِقٍ اِذَا وَقَبَ ۞
وَمِنْ شَرِّ النَّفّٰثٰتِ فِي الْعُقَدِ ۞
وَمِنْ شَرِّ حَاسِدٍ اِذَا حَسَدَ ۞

In the name of Allah,
the Compassionate, the Merciful.

Say: 'I take refuge with the
Lord of the daybreak
from the evil of what He has created,
from the evil of darkness when it gathers,
from the evil of those who blow on knots,
from the evil of an envier when he envies.'

# Surah An-Nas

**MEN**

سُوْرَةُ النَّاسِ

بِسْمِ اللّٰهِ الرَّحْمٰنِ الرَّحِيْمِ

قُلْ أَعُوْذُ بِرَبِّ النَّاسِ ۙ

مَلِكِ النَّاسِ ۙ إِلٰهِ النَّاسِ ۙ

مِنْ شَرِّ الْوَسْوَاسِ ۙ الْخَنَّاسِ ۙ

الَّذِيْ يُوَسْوِسُ فِيْ صُدُوْرِ النَّاسِ ۙ

مِنَ الْجِنَّةِ وَالنَّاسِ ۚ

In the name of Allah,
the Compassionate, the Merciful.

Say: I take refuge with the Lord of men,
the King of men, the God of men
from the evil of those who whisper,
who whisper in human hearts;
from jinn and men.

# Children's Books

### Quran Stories for Little Hearts
- THE MORALS OF BELIEVERS
- THE MIRACULOUS BABY
- THE PROPHET AND THE BLIND MAN
- THE TREASURE HOUSE

### Prophet Muhammad for Little Hearts
- AN EXTRAORDINARY EXPERIENCE
- PROPHET OF PEACE

### Ramadan and Eid Stories
- Aminah and Aisha's EID GIFTS
- EID KAREEM Ameen Sahh!

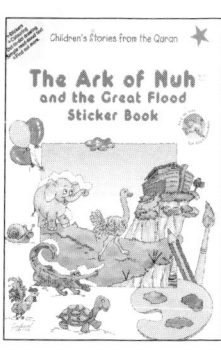

### Children's Stories from the Quran
- The Ark of Nuh and the Great Flood Sticker Book

### The Junior Encyclopaedia of Islam

- My Egyptian Village

### Garden of Islam
- OWL AND THE DAWN PRAYER
- THE CAMEL'S JOURNEY

- My Palestinian Village

### Quran Stories for Young Readers
- The Camel and the Evil People
- Prophet Muhammad Receives the First Revelation
- The Most Honorable Woman
- The Tribe of Quraysh
- The Army Walks Through the Valley

# Gift Boxes

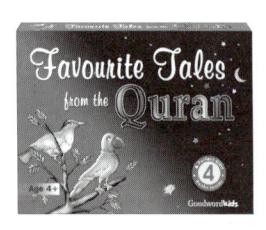

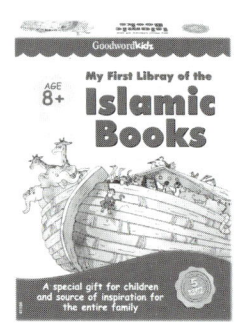